autumn 2015

Mission

We understand "community literacy" as the domain for literacy work that exists outside of mainstream educational and work institutions. It can be found in programs devoted to adult education, early childhood education, reading initiatives, lifelong learning, workplace literacy, or work with marginalized populations, but it can also be found in more informal, ad hoc projects.

For us, literacy is defined as the realm where attention is paid not just to content or to knowledge but to the symbolic means by which it is represented and used. Thus, literacy makes reference not just to letters and to text but to other multimodal and technological representations as well. We publish work that contributes to the field's emerging methodologies and research agendas.

Subscriptions

We are pleased to offer subscriptions to CLJ—two issues per year:

Institutions & libraries	$200.00
Faculty	$35.00
Graduate students & community workers	$20.00
International Shipping	$10.00

Please send a check or money order made out to the University of Arizona Foundation to:

John Warnock, *Community Literacy Journal*
445 Modern Languages Bldg., University of Arizona, P.O. Box 210067
Tucson, AZ 85721
Info: johnw@u.arizona.edu

Cover Art

Photograph: "Pane di Altamura," by Aimée Knight.

> Aimée Knight is an assistant professor in the Communication Studies Department at Saint Joseph's University. Her research centers on multimodal composition and visual and cultural rhetorics. This photo was taken during a Digital Storytelling workshop she co-led in Altamura, Italy in June 2014. During the hands-on workshop participants made cheese by traditional methods, sampled olive oils in the grove, dined in fields, beaches and star-lit courtyards, rose early to bake crusty bread in the town oven and danced to tambourines. This photo features Pane di Altamura, a regional bread that has changed little in over 2000 years. A small but committed community of bakers continues to bake Pane di Altamura employing traditional ingredients and methods.

Editorial Advisory Board

Jonathan Alexander	University of California, Irvine
Nancy Guerra Barron	Northern Arizona University
David Barton	Lancaster University, UK
David Blakesley	Clemson University
Melody Bowdon	University of Central Florida
Tara Brabazon	University of Brighton, UK
Danika Brown	University of Texas–Pan American
Ernesto Cardenal	Casa de los Tres Mundos, Managua
Marilyn Cooper	Michigan Technological University
Linda Flower	Carnegie Mellon University
Diana George	Virginia Tech University
Jeff Grabill	Michigan State University
Greg Hart	Tucson Area Literacy Coalition
Shirley Brice Heath	Stanford University
Tobi Jacobi	Colorado State University
Lou Johnson	River Parishes YMCA, New Orleans
Paula Mathieu	Boston College
Regina Mokgokong	Project Literacy, Pretoria, South Africa
Ruth E. Ray	Wayne State University
Georgia Rhoades	Appalachian State University
Mike Rose	University of California, Los Angeles
Tiffany Rousculp	Salt Lake Community College
Cynthia Selfe	The Ohio State University
Tanya Shuy	U.S. Department of Education
Vanderlei de Souza	Faculdade de Tecnologia de Indaiatuba, São Paulo
John Trimbur	Worcester Polytechnic Institute
Christopher Wilkey	Northern Kentucky University

COMMUNITY LITERACY Journal

Editors	Michael R. Moore DePaul University
	John Warnock University of Arizona
Senior Assistant Editor	Amanda Gaddam DePaul University
Assistant Editors	Mariana Grohowski Massachusetts Maritime Academy
	Alexandra Nates-Perez DePaul University
Copy Editors	Jake Dinneen DePaul University
	Brandon Haskey DePaul University
	Mark Lazio DePaul University
	James Neisen DePaul University
	Margaret Poncin DePaul University
	Bridget Wagner DePaul University
Journal Manager	Daniel James Carroll DePaul University
Design & Production Editor	Aim Larrabee DePaul University
Book & New Media Review Editor	Jessica Shumake University of Arizona
Social Media Editor	Melissa Pompos University of Central Florida
Consulting Editors	Eric Plattner DePaul University
	Stephanie Vie Fort Lewis College
	Maria Conti Univerity of Arizona

Submissions

The peer-reviewed *Community Literacy Journal* seeks contributions for upcoming issues. We welcome submissions that address social, cultural, rhetorical, or institutional aspects of community literacy; we particularly welcome pieces authored in collaboration with community partners.

Manuscripts should be submitted according to the standards of the *MLA Handbook for Writers of Research Papers*, 7th ed. (New York: MLA).

Shorter and longer pieces are acceptable (8–25 manuscript pages) depending on authors' approaches. Case studies, reflective pieces, scholarly articles, etc., are all welcome.

To submit manuscripts, visit our site—communityliteracy.org—and register as an author. Send queries to Michael Moore: mmoore46@depaul.edu.

Advertising

The Community Literacy Journal welcomes advertising. The journal is published twice annually, in the Fall and Spring (Nov. and Mar.). Deadlines for advertising are two months prior to publication (Sept. and Jan.).

Ad Sizes and Pricing

Half page (trim size 6X4.5)	$200
Full page (trim size 6X9)	$350
Inside back cover (trim size 6X9)	$500
Inside front cover (trim size 6X9)	$600

Format

We accept .PDF, .JPG, .TIF or .EPS. All advertising images should be camera-ready and have a minimum resolution of 300 DPI. For more information, please contact Michael Moore: mmoore46@depaul.edu.

Copyright © 2015 *Community Literacy Journal*
ISSN 1555-9734

Community Literacy Journal is a member of the Council of Editors of Learned Journals

Printing and distribution managed by Parlor Press.

ptumn 2015

COMMUNITY LITERACY Journal

Autumn 2015
Volume 10 Issue 1

Special Issue: Community Food Literacies

Table of Contents

Articles

Community Food Literacies: An Introduction..1
Michael Pennell

Nutritional Noise: Community Literacies and the Movement
Against Foods Labeled as "Natural"...4
Erin Trauth

De aquí y de allá: Changing Perceptions of Literacy through
Food Pedagogy, Asset-Based Narratives, and Hybrid Spaces.......................21
*Lucía Durá, Consuelo Salas, William Medina-Jerez,
and Virgina Hill*

Mindful Persistence: Literacies for Taking Up and Sustaining
Fermented-Food Products..40
*Christina Santana, Stacey Kuznetsov, Sheri Schmeckpeper,
Linda J. Curry, Elenore Long, Lauren Davis, Heidi Koerner,
and Kimberly Butterfield McQuarrie*

Sponsors of Agricultural Literacies: Intersections of Institutional
and Local Knowledge in a Farming Community...59
Marcy L. Galbreath

Community Cookbooks: Sponsors of Literacy and Community
Identity..73
Lisa Mastrangelo

Feed Your Mind: Cultivating Ecological Community Literacies
with Permaculture..87
Stephanie Wade

Book & New Media Reviews

From the Book & New Media Review Editor's Desk 101
Jessica Shumake
Ryan Cresawn and Saul Hernandez, Interns

Keyword Essay: "Selfie"..103
Amanda Fields and Melanie Carter

Transiciones: Pathways of Latinas and Latinos Writing in High School and College
By Todd Ruecker..112
Reviewed by Brad Jacobson

Negotiating a Perilous Empowerment: Appalachian Women's Literacies
By Erica Abrams Locklear..117
Reviewed by Jessica Pauszek

Producing Good Citizens: Literacy Training in Anxious Times
By Amy J. Wan...122
Reviewed by Daniel Bernal

Creating Effective Community Partnerships for School Improvement: A Guide for School Leaders
By Hazel M. Carter...127
Reviewed by Erika Dyk

Community Food Literacies: An Introduction

Michael Pennell, Special Guest Editor

> Because food sovereignty and food justice are some of the most important issues of our time, issues that tie to topics of ecological collapse, peak oil, racism, poverty, corporate capitalism, overpopulation, disease, and hunger, service-learning practitioners are well-positioned to help launch initiatives in colleges and universities across the country, in partnership with our local communities, to address community-centered food literacy (4).
>
> Veronica House

This special issue of the *Community Literacy Journal*, focused on community food literacies, presents six responses to and extensions of Veronica House's call for service-learning practitioners and, more generally, literacy workers across communities and educational institutions. This journal provides an ideal venue within which to grapple with the overlapping and intertwined relationship between food and literacy, especially as it relates to communities. Both food and literacy find themselves in equally "revolutionary" stages of their development. While the literacy revolution may be found in discussions of a rise in social media, mobile communication devices, and ubiquitous network technologies, the food revolution is witnessed in a re-localization of food systems, including farmers markets, community-supported agriculture, and community gardens. Moreover, both "revolutionary" moments present challenges, concerns, and inequalities, captured in discussions of digital divides, cyber-security, labor, food deserts, hunger, and sustainability. The recent local food movements are tied to and reflective of local communities. In particular, these local communities represent the people, places, and literacies behind our food system. Furthermore, they occupy a key context for investigating and exploring the intertwining of food and community literacy. The growing overlaps and complicated relationships between food and literacy warrant a special issue devoted to these expanding relationships.

The following articles present a variety of perspectives on community food literacies, ranging from inside and outside educational institutions. All of the authors echo House's call for investigating and acting on community food literacies, as well as highlight her positioning of service-learning, rhetoric and composition instructors, and literacy workers in general, as key allies and advocates for such a focus on community food literacies. Ideally, this collection will strengthen and/or encourage fellow literacy workers to unpack and explore the complicated pairing of food and literacy in our communities, workplaces, and classrooms.

In literacy and food discussions, how we label and define practices and products is a key window into the evolving food movement. For example, discussions surround such questions as: What is "local"? What is the difference between organic and natural? What does it mean for an animal to be "cage free"? Erin Trauth, in her article, "Nutritional Noise: Community Literacies and the Movement Against Foods Labeled as 'Natural,'" explores the ubiquity of "natural" as a label for food and food production practices. She examines how the label is deployed in an expanding market of "natural foods," along with a growing grassroots movement challenging the use of "natural." Trauth supplements her discussion by presenting survey data capturing participants' understandings of "natural" and natural foods.

Moving into the spaces within which we connect food and literacy education, Lucia Dura, Consuelo Salas, William Medina-Jerez, and Virginia Hill offer an overview of an interdisciplinary, inter-institutional, after-school literacy partnership on the U.S.-Mexico border. Their article, "*De aquí y de allá*: Changing Perceptions of Literacy through Food Pedagogy, Asset-Based Narratives, and Hybrid Spaces," shares how the Escuelita Program uses food pedagogy to tap into funds of knowledge, bridging "home" and "school" literacies.

Similarly investigating the spaces within which community food literacies develop and impact our lives, Christina Santana, Stacey Kuznetsov, Sheri Schmeckpeper, Linda Curry, Elenore Long, Lauren Davis, Heidi Koerner, and Kimberly McQuarrie, show how "mindful persistence" is central to a team of scholars' and community members' exposure to and interest in fermentation-based food projects. As the article, "Mindful Persistence: Literacies for Taking up and Sustaining Fermented-Food Projects," highlights, an interest in fermentation does not require or assume identical understandings of the science of fermentation or similar positions in the probiotic debate surrounding contemporary fermentation practices.

In continuing to explore our understanding of key concepts in the development of community food literacies, Marcy Galbreath examines oral histories and archival materials to see how agricultural literacy, arising in the scientific research of land-grant colleges, was transmitted to local farming communities. In particular, the article, titled "Sponsors of Agricultural Literacies: Intersections of Institutional and Local Knowledge in a Farming Community," captures the role of extension services and 4-H programs in interfacing with local farming communities.

A focus on archival materials continues with Lisa Mastrangelo's "Community Cookbooks: Sponsors of Literacy and Community Identity." In her contribution, Mastrangelo investigates how communities are created by and reflected in the shared memories/traditions, geographical identifications, and representations of class within two cookbooks. With the proliferation of both community and celebrity cookbooks in our current food movement, we would be wise to follow Mastrangelo's lead in unpacking such print and digital books.

Echoing and expanding the call forwarded by Veronica House, Stephanie Wade places our attention back on the role of the classroom and our pedagogies in analyzing and engaging with local food literacies. Her article, "Feed Your Mind: Cultivating Ecological Community Literacies with Permaculture," asks writing and rhetoric teachers to push their use of ecological literacies by practicing permaculture, an ecological alternative to conventional agriculture. Her work shares ecological community literacy projects created by students grounded in the concept of permaculture.

Finally, I draw your attention back to the cover image. This image of the cutting of bread, specifically, *Pane di Altamura*, was provided generously by Aimée Knight. From the individual to institutional level, we are all implicated in and exposed to the food and literacy "revolutions"; more importantly, how we respond to, invest in, and enact such revolutions in our families, neighborhoods, and workplaces will determine how such revolutions evolve for future communities. Intervening in community food literacies requires an understanding of process, not just product. The hands that cut the bread, as in the cover image, represent one moment in an extensive process, a process of food and literacy.

Works Cited

House, Veronica. "Re-Framing the Argument: Critical Service-Learning and Community-Centered Food Literacy." *Community Literacy Journal* 8.2 (Spring 2014): 1-16.

Nutritional Noise: Community Literacies and the Movement Against Foods Labeled as "Natural"

Erin Trauth

In the face of the $44 billion market—and rising—for foods labeled as "natural" (despite any formal regulatory oversight on the use of this term), this article examines multiple complex layers of community literacies and movements involving foods labeled as "natural," including an increasing availability of "natural" foods and simultaneous rise in U.S. obesity rates, as well as grassroots movements that have challenged the use of "natural." Then, using an online survey of 707 respondents in a localized community setting, I provide my own examination of literacies of "natural" foods by assessing specific consumer interpretations and regulatory knowledge of the word "natural" as it is found on food labels. Ultimately, I discuss what role these varying levels of literacies play in the rising U.S. movement to push back against the use of this claim in the face of an otherwise flourishing "natural" food market.

Background: Food Labels and the "Natural" Food Movement

Americans are increasingly growing more concerned about their food. According to a 2014 report from the U.S. Department of Agriculture's Economic Research Service, American adults are making marked attempts to "eat better, make better use of available nutrition information, consume fewer calories coming from fat and saturated fat, and consume less cholesterol and eat more fiber" than they were 10 years ago (par. 1). In addition, American concern with the origins and ingredients of food has grown; this increased interest in "healthier" foods, often centered on consuming fewer chemical/processed ingredients and higher levels of "natural" ingredients, can be noted through the increased availability of supermarkets and restaurants boasting an array of "natural" selections. While the "natural" foods offered to consumers are often labeled with many different terms, from "smart choice" to "free range" to "good for you," no other label claim, in recent years, has faced the simultaneous levels of attention and scrutiny as "natural."

The word "natural," and its variations—i.e. "all natural" and "made with natural ingredients"—as they are used on United States food labels, have been major marketing assets to the food industry over the past several years. At the same time, they have also been key points of contention for consumers, as U.S. obesity rates continue to rise and grassroots campaigns expose the claim that the word is merely marketing language, prompting numerous community efforts to eradicate its use. From 2012 to 2013, consumers spent more than $44 billion on food products labeled specifically as "natural." A recent study also claims that 51 percent of Americans seek out products labeled as "natural" when they are grocery shopping (Esterl par. 4). The claim is so popular that foods labeled "natural" made up approximately 10 percent of the grocery sales in 2013 (Cummins par. 1). A 2009 study by The Shelton Group found that "natural" is the sole most popular claim with consumers, and the "Clean Label Study" of 2012 found that 74 percent of consumers think "natural" foods are healthier (Food Navigator par. 2).

However, despite this rise in demand for "natural" foods as part of the healthy-eating movement, we have also seen a steady rise in obesity rates (Tierney 1). Many call this part of the "American obesity paradox," which shows a coincident rise in the U.S. obesity rate and demand for "healthier" foods (Tierney 1). One essence of this phenomenon is that consumers are reaching for "healthier" foods by way of eating foods with a "natural" label, and this may cause a "halo" effect surrounding the food (Tierney 2), meaning consumers will often overestimate the healthfulness of a food if a label claim is given, i.e. "low fat" or "natural." Researchers have found that people will then eat more of this product because they think it is healthier. In the case of foods labeled as "natural," this paradox is particularly important to examine, since the term faces no formal regulation and may entice people to eat more of a product they think is healthier—but in fact may be no better than the more obviously unhealthy selections not labeled as "natural."

Further complicating the complex issues already at hand, in the background of the concurrent boom of "natural" products and obesity rates, another countermovement reflecting a dissatisfaction with the regulation of "natural" products has also emerged in local communities. A 2006 poll by Harris Interactive found that "when asked whether the government should provide food manufacturers with regulations to follow when making a 'natural' claim, 83% answered 'yes' that the government should provide such regulations" (The Sugar Association 9). In addition to these sentiments being expressed, community movements to push back against the use of this term on food labels—from online petitions to lawsuits against food companies—have sprung up across the country.

On the surface, many different movements are at play in the "natural" food arena, demonstrating numerous diverse community literacies about these foods. On the one hand, a movement exists in the United States to purchase seemingly healthier foods, and, from the aforementioned statistics about the rise of natural food purchases, the "natural" phrase seems to entice consumers, which many equate to "healthier" eating. This demonstrates, at the very least, a baseline literacy about the benefits of eating healthier and marked attempts to do so. At the same time, the fact that the former group focuses on purchasing "natural" products when they are virtually unregulated may indicate a deficient literacy exists about the true nature of many marketing health claims made on food products, especially "natural." On the other hand, a coincidental growing community movement has pushed back against the food industry and the Food and Drug Administration (FDA) about the term "natural," demonstrating an opposing community literacy about the true meaning behind unregulated food label language.

All of these issues present a need for further examination of this topic: how far apart are these community groups in their literacies about "natural" foods? What role does consumer literacy about "natural" foods play in local community efforts to push back against this food label claim? To what degree does literacy about the unregulated nature of these foods exist? What, if anything, has been impacted by grassroots community efforts to increase other consumers' knowledge about the true nature of "natural" foods and to influence the Food and Drug Administration's (FDA) decision-making? In a sample community, just how literate are consumers about the "natural" term? For those consumers who are buying food labeled as "natural," do they feel "natural" products will provide them with specific positive nutritional benefits, such as improved health and/or a reduced risk of disease? What, exactly, do they think this means about the food product in terms of ingredients and nutritional value? Do they think this claim is regulated by the FDA or not? How do members of a sample community make their own meaning amidst the "nutritional noise," or, all the complex layers of understanding surrounding "natural" foods?

In this article, I further investigate these important questions and subsequently examine the complex movements surrounding "natural" food and varying community literacies. I first provide an overview of the FDA's current definition—as of May 2015—of "natural." Then, I describe grassroots community movements that have challenged the use of this word on food labels and demonstrated a movement to make these issues more publically known, including online petitions and lawsuits against food companies using this phrase on its labels, and how the FDA has responded to some of these community movements. Then, using a survey of 707 respondents in a localized community setting, I provide my own examination of literacy of "natural" foods by assessing consumer interpretations and regulatory knowledge of the word "natural" as it is found on food labels. Using this sample, I discuss the interpretations of and literacy about "natural" as it is currently used on the front of food packaging and what potential role this knowledge (or lack thereof) plays in the movement to further regulate this term in the context of a rising global movement to better understand what is in our food.

Defining "Natural" on U.S. Food Labels: The FDA and Baseline Consumer Perceptions

The FDA's Stance. Despite its widespread use on food labels, the term "natural" as it applies in the United States is an arguable declaration. Unlike the term "organic," "natural" currently faces no true directive by the FDA, the main source of governance for U.S. food corporations and their use of food labels. Thus far, the FDA "has not developed a definition for use of the term natural or its derivatives" and only states that it "has not objected to the use of the term if the food does not contain added color, artificial flavors, or synthetic substances" (FDA par. 5). William Sears, M.D., an Associate Clinical Professor of Pediatrics at the University of California-Irvine School of Medicine, makes a case that the word is deceptive:

> 'Natural' is probably the least trustworthy of all the label terms. While the term 'natural' sounds appealing, it really says little about the nutritional quality of the food, or even its safety. In reality, 'natural' is empty of nutritional meaning. Consumers believe that 'natural' means the food is pretty much as Mother Nature grew it, but this is seldom the case (par. 3).

Because the FDA has not taken any formal regulatory stance on the word, the use of it is often found on food labels with little (if any) meaning about the product itself, unless accompanied by a regulated "organic" symbol (Sears par. 4).

What Consumers Think 'Natural' Means. Although the word is not formally defined, the larger U.S. community does have some baseline ideas about what the word *should* mean. In a 2014 survey conducted by the Consumer Reports National Research Center, U.S. consumers believe the "natural" label should mean, "no pesticides were used (86%), no artificial ingredients were used (86%), no artificial materials were used during processing (87%), and no genetically-modified organisms (GMOs) were used (85%)" (8). A 2006 Harris Interactive poll of 1000 respondents found that "eighty-five percent of 1000 people surveyed said that they would not consider any food containing; anything artificial or synthetic to be natural. Consumers also agreed that the amount of processing (52%) and/or altering of raw materials (60%) should disqualify a product from making a 'natural' claim" (The Sugar Association 9). Later in this article, I will provide the results of my own inquiry into a localized community's assessments through open-ended consumer definitions of the word "natural," evaluations as to whether such a term would mean that a food could improve health or reduce risk of disease, and understanding of the term's regulation or lack thereof. First, I will describe several widespread public community movements to extend individual literacy into social action via attempts to influence the FDA's decision-making.

Community Movements to Regulate "Natural"

A growing movement claims that the FDA should create formal definitions of "natural" which are supported by scientific backing, as opposed to allowing for the use of what many in this movement deep as ambiguous and/or misleading (TakePart 1). Others in this movement assert that if the FDA cannot settle on a definition and regulatory mandate for "natural," then companies should be barred from using the term altogether (TakePart 1). While the arguments take on different degrees of proposed action, community movements demonstrating a counter literacy about the unregulated nature of "natural" have gained traction, even in the face of the soaring $44 billion "natural" food market.

Petitions. Despite the lack of regulation surrounding the word "natural" as it is used on food labels, there is a movement counter to that of the otherwise positive response to "natural" foods (as evidenced by the $44 billion-and-rising market) taking its own steps to convince the FDA to further define or even outright ban the use of the word on food labels. In 2015, a TakePart petition titled "Stop Confusing Consumers: Ban the 'Natural' Label" received over 33,000 signatures. In it, respondents urged both the FDA and the USDA to ban and/or restrict its use on food products. In a similar move, consumers attempted to start a movement on Change.org in 2014. In this petition's language, the petition organizer writes: "Please FDA and USDA: create a definition in line with what the general public thinks of the word natural. Create a definition for the use of the word natural on food labels. I no longer want to be misled about what I am putting in my body" (Change.org par. 5). A Care2 petition sponsored by Consumersunion.org, titled "Tell the FDA to Be Honest with Food Labeling" currently has more than 130,000 signatures (as of May 2015). The petition urges respondents to "Tell the FDA to strike a blow for truth in labeling and drop the misleading 'natural' label from food once and for all!" As of May 2015, the campaign was shared on Facebook nearly 5000 times with thousands of in-support comments following.

Action in the Courts. In the face of the current lack of definition and regulation of "natural" and consumers' specific notions about the meanings and use of "natural" on food labels, some litigators have claimed that the FDA and USDA are "sleeping on the job": Nicole E. Negowetti, Assistant Professor of Law at Valparaiso University Law School, argues: "although both the FDA and USDA are statutorily mandated to protect consumer interests by prohibiting false and misleading labeling, both agencies have refused to formally define the term" (582). She explains, that due to "consumers' inherent lack of knowledge about food ingredients, food technology, food ingredient terminology" they are bound to face difficulty when trying to discern if a product is actually "natural" (20). Therefore, she asserts, "consumers should be able to rely on the oversight of regulatory agencies to provide food manufacturers with clear and concise regulations" (20).

Beyond grassroots attempts to petition companies, consumers have also taken action against the use of "natural" in the courts. Since 2007, class action lawsuits have been launched against companies such as Bear Naked, Pepperidge Farm, Frito-Lay, Pepsico, Kashi, Kellogg's, Snapple, ConAgra, Arizona, and General Mills by consumers related to the use of "natural" claims made on each company's products in some form. From 2011 to 2013, at least 100 lawsuits involving the "natural" claim were seen by the court system (Esterl par. 8). In most cases, according to Negowetti, the suits claim that "natural" marketing claims "violate state consumer protection statutes that proscribe false and misleading advertising" (21).

In these lawsuits, consumers are publically exhibiting an attempt to make the food industry take notice of their literacy about "natural" foods in a tangible way and exerting effort to help alter the "natural" foods landscape. However, the results of these attempts in the courtroom thus far have been mixed. Jennifer L. Pomeranz, Assistant Professor of Public Health at Temple University, explains that several courts have "dismissed natural claims based on the doctrine of primary jurisdiction or stayed the case to seek clarification from the FDA, even though the Agency repeatedly declines to intervene or further define the term" (439). There has been some success with settlements: Barbara's Bakery, maker of Puffins cereal, and PepsiCo, which owns Naked Juice, each settled respective claims for $4 million and $9 million (Pomeranz 440). In 2008, the Ninth Circuit found that Gerber's fruit snacks marketed as natural would "likely deceive a reasonable consumer" because "the packaging pictures a number of different fruits, potentially suggesting (falsely) that those fruits or their juices are contained in the product" (Williams vs. Gerber 2008). The court found that "reasonable consumers should [not] be expected to look beyond misleading representations on the front of the box to discover the truth from the ingredient list ... on the side of the box." (Williams vs. Gerber 2008).

Perhaps the most interesting impact of the suits, however, is that many food makers have "reportedly started to pull the natural claim, especially when they use GMOs, due to the influx of litigation and the uncertainty of the FDA's position" (Pomeranz 440). This movement by the food industry indicates, at the very least, some companies may be taking notice of the rising literacy about "natural" foods consumers are exhibiting.

The FDA Responds. In January 2014, the FDA responded to a case in which "three separate US.S. District Court cases—Cox v. Gruma Corp. (N.D. Cal.), Barnes v. Campbell Soup Co. (N.D. Cal.), and In Re General Mills, Inc. Kix Cereal Litigation (D.N.J.)"—called upon the organization to determine whether or not food products containing genetically modified ingredients (GMO) could be labeled "natural" (Fogel par. 2). Many claim the FDA's response to this call would set a precedent for how the organization would move forward with generally regulating the "natural" food market (not just GMO foods) (TakePart 1).

In response to this call, the FDA "respectfully declined" to determine if GMO foods should be permitted to be labeled as "natural." In a letter response, Leslie Kux, assistant commissioner for Policy for the FDA, wrote:

> If FDA were inclined to revoke, amend, or add to this policy [its definition of 'natural'], we would likely embark on a public process, such as issuing a regulation or formal guidance, in order to determine whether to make such a change; we would not do so in the context of litigation between private properties (2).

Kux also noted "any definition of natural on food labeling has implications well beyond the narrow scope of genetically engineered food ingredients" (2). She wrote that the FDA has been "considering the issue" with the USDA, another stakeholder in the "natural" labeling context, but there is "no assurance that we would revoke, amend, or add to the current policy, or develop any definition at all" (2).

The letter asserts that the FDA is attending to "priority food public health and safety matters" for now. In addition, the FDA claimed that the public would have to be engaged at a deeper level, despite all of the petitioning and lawsuits, to understand consumer "perceptions and beliefs" about the term "natural" and the issue of further defining and/or regulating it (2).

As a start to this call to more deeply understand consumer perceptions and contribute insights to at least one layer of the complex puzzle surrounding "natural" foods, in the following section, I provide the results of a large-scale survey, in which I sought to understand how a localized community construes the word "natural" on current front-of-package labels. Further, in this sample, I demonstrate the sampled community's literacy about whether or not "natural" products are regulated by the FDA in a given community. Then, I discuss what potential role this knowledge (or lack thereof) can play in the movement to further understand the complex issue of understanding consumers and regulating "natural" label claims.

"Natural" Interpretations and Community Literacy: A Survey of 707 Respondents

In my own exploration of consumer literacy regarding the "natural" food label claim, I sought to understand how a sample of respondents within a local community construes the word "natural" on current front-of-package labels. In this work, I add to the conversation in the greater movement to understand how "natural" is understood, defined, and interpreted at a qualitative level, thus providing a snapshot of one sample community's literacy of this topic. In the following section, before moving on to a discussion of my results, I provide a brief summary of my study's methods for this specific assessment of consumer literacy about "natural" foods.

Methods Summary. For this project, I used a large-scale survey of students currently attending the University of Colorado-Colorado Springs. At the time of this project, which began in November 2013, I was an instructor at this university and was able to distribute the survey anonymously via the student email mailing list. Over the course of a one-month period, 707 students completed my survey. When all 707 responses were compiled, I used Survey Monkey online survey tools to first compile total average results for every question, which includes demographic inquiries, questions about concerns for future health issues, assessments of current food label interpretations, questions regarding concern with purchasing healthy foods, and then open-ended and Likert-scale questions regarding the "natural" claim. The core questions were intended to measure respondents' initial interpretations of what the claims said about the food product's nutritional value and ingredients. Then, I assessed consumer confidence in the product's ability to improve health or prevent disease, followed by a question as to whether or not respondents believed the claims were authorized for use by the FDA or not. The participants' understanding of regulation of the front-of-package label claims was measured by the response to a yes/no question each respondent answered in the survey that they could either get right or wrong whether or not a claim is authorized for use by the FDA. These responses served as the gauge for understanding for regulation, and, thus, literacy about regulation, of the tested "natural" claim.

My sample for the survey is the result of a convenience sampling method. I used my connection as an instructor on the University of Colorado-Colorado Springs campus to disseminate my electronic survey to the student population. As an instructor, I had access to the university's student e-mail list. The student e-mail list has been designed so that no individual email addresses or names are revealed, and no individual persons were contacted. Full university Institutional Review Board approval was granted for this study. The survey submissions were stored in one Survey Monkey account for the duration of the study and were protected via a secure password-protected connection and account. Compensation for this survey was entrance into a random drawing for one $25 Chipotle gift card. One respondent won this card and was contacted via email only for the purpose of obtaining information to mail the gift card. The explanation of the survey and its purposes along with a link was sent via this e-mail list on November 5, 2013 and was open for exactly one month until December 5, 2013.

The sample yielded 707 responses from a range of students at the University of Colorado—Colorado Springs (UCCS). The UCCS student population provided a wide range of responses, as the campus is a mix of traditional and non-traditional undergraduate and graduate students with varying backgrounds and geographic origins. In fall 2013, UCCS enrolled 10,619 total students, 40% of whom were first-generation students (UCCS Institutional Research, 2013). Twenty-two percent of these students were of minority ethnicities, and 30% received Pell Grant scholarships. The average age of undergraduate students was 23.2 and, for graduate students, 33.5. Table 1 shows the enrollment and class breakdown of UCCS students from 2010 - Fall 2013.

Table 1: UCCS Student Class Level, 2010- Fall 2013 (UCCS Institutional Research)

Source: UCCS Institutional Research, University of Colorado-Colorado Springs. 2013. Web. Nov. 2014.

Academic Level	2010 Census	2010 EOT	2011 Census	2011 EOT	2012 Census	2012 EOT	2013 Census	2013 EOT
Freshman	1899	1826	2171	2111	2336	2291	2493	2472
Sophomore	1468	1472	1481	1484	1651	1682	1794	1793
Junior	1508	1541	1660	1668	1717	1699	1883	1888
Senior	1548	1567	1594	1610	1682	1711	1820	1835
Senior Fifth Year	661	682	678	718	691	700	792	813
Graduate	1546	1556	1478	1492	1480	1502	1580	1589
Unclassified	262	256	259	256	220	213	236	229
Total	8892	8900	9321	9339	9777	9798	10598	10619

After compiling the 707 total responses, I first used my survey platform to determine basic information about the total respondent population, including demographic information, basic health background, reports of prior use of food labels, perceived respondent shopping preferences—i.e., how often they reportedly seek to buy healthy foods. In the following section, I will describe the results of this study of community interpretations of the "natural" claim.

Key Findings. In the following section, I provide the results of the sample population's interpretation and literacy about "natural" as it is used on U.S. front-of-package food labels.

In response to the question "**When you see the word 'natural' on a front-of-package label, what does this mean to you about the overall nutritional value of the product?**" respondents provided a range of responses. Textual analysis yielded the most common responses as follows in table 2:

Table 2: Textual Analysis of Open-Ended Responses to "Natural" Nutritional Value	
Number of Respondents (percent of sample)	Textual Response
120 respondents (17 percent)	it means "nothing" about the nutritional value of the product.
69 respondents (8 percent)	the product would have a higher nutritional value.
69 respondents (8 percent)	the product would be less processed.
48 respondents (5 percent)	the product would be healthier.
46 respondents (5 percent)	the product would contain fewer chemicals.
44 respondents (5 percent)	the product may be organic or contain organic ingredients.
32 respondents (3 percent)	the product may contain fewer preservatives.
16 respondents (1 percent)	the product could be more nutritious.

Some open-ended text responses indicate knowledge of the use of marketing terms on food labels, i.e.: "It means absolutely nothing. Natural is a buzz-word. It could be worse or better for me" and "This makes my eyebrows raise. It seems like this is a product that I will want to investigate more. I will likely pick up this product and read the ingredients to check for preservatives and chemical additives. If it has none of these, I may purchase the product."

On the other hand, other responses exhibit the perception that a food with a "natural" label is indeed different than foods not labeled with the word and its variations—i.e. "The nutritional value is higher than products without this label" and "The nutritional value is higher than the non-natural products".

Other common responses indicate the product would be sold at a higher cost than its counterparts: "This product will have similar or less ingredients for an increased cost." Others thought the product would be marketed to certain groups of people or simply meant "good marketing" but did not mean much about the product itself: "Natural products seem to be oriented towards people who are 'green'. I do not believe that there is a huge difference between products that are and are not labeled this way;" "It means the manufacturer seeks to provide an image of health and avoidance of artificial ingredients;" and "That they've got a good marketing and design team and rarely means anything."

Table 3: Textual Analysis of Open-Ended Responses to "Natural" Ingredients	
Number of Respondents (percent of sample)	Textual Response
92 respondents (13 percent)	the product would be less processed.
85 respondents (12 percent)	this meant "nothing" about the ingredients of the product.
83 respondents (10 percent)	the product would contain fewer chemicals
63 respondents (7 percent)	the product might contain organic ingredients, or ingredients regulated to the organic standard.
63 respondents (7 percent)	the product would contain fewer preservatives.
31 respondents (3 percent)	the product would contain fewer artificial ingredients.
24 respondents (2 percent)	the product would be "healthy."
21 respondents (2 percent)	the product would contain fewer pesticides.
19 respondents (2 percent)	the product would contain fewer additives.
11 respondents (1 percent)	the product would contain fewer artificial growth hormones.
10 respondents (1 percent)	the product would be unprocessed.
10 respondents (1 percent)	the product would not contain genetically modified ingredients.
9 respondents (1 percent)	the product would be "healthier."

Regarding the question "When you see the word 'natural' on a front-of-package label, what does this mean to you about the ingredients of the product?" textual analysis yielded the following results:

Other responses noted a lack of "lab" ingredients, "synthetic" ingredients, "extra" ingredients, and "man-made" ingredients. Others also noted the product would be of "higher quality" and made of "good ingredients." Many respondents noted a tie to nature, i.e. "To me, it means that it contains ingredients that occur in nature. There is nothing man-made in it like artificial sweeteners, colors, fillers, preservatives."

Regarding confidence in the suggestion that a product labeled as "natural" will help improve one's health, over 30% of respondents note that they are very confident or somewhat confident: 4.5% of respondents note that they are very confident and 26.4% are somewhat confident. Over 35% note they were neutral on the matter. The final third, 32.2% of respondents, note they are somewhat unconfident or very unconfident: 20.2 %, or 143 respondents are somewhat unconfident and 12% of respondents are very unconfident in the food product's ability to improve health. A full distribution of these responses is shown in figure 1.

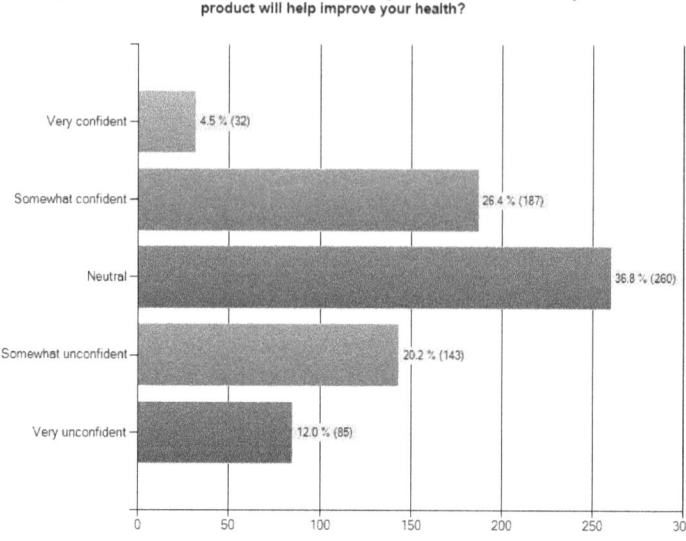

Figure 1: Respondent Confidence in "Natural" Foods' Ability to Improve Health

The mean response to this question was "neutral," and the mode is also "neutral."

Table 4: Respondent Confidence in "Natural" Foods' Ability to Improve Health, Mean Response			
Response	Score	Percent Response	Average (Mean)
Very Confident	5	4.5%	0.23
Somewhat Confident	4	26.3%	1.05
Neutral	3	**36.8%**	**1.10**
Somewhat Unconfident	2	20.2%	0.40
Very Unconfident	1	12.0%	0.12
		99.8%	2.91

Regarding confidence in the suggestion that a product labeled as "natural" will help prevent the risk of potential disease, nearly one quarter of respondents combined note that they are very confident or somewhat confident: 3% are very confident, and 21.4% are somewhat confident. Nearly 40 % note they are neutral on the matter. More than 35 percent note they are somewhat unconfident or very unconfident: 20.7 % are somewhat unconfident, and 15.1% are very unconfident in the food product's ability to improve health.

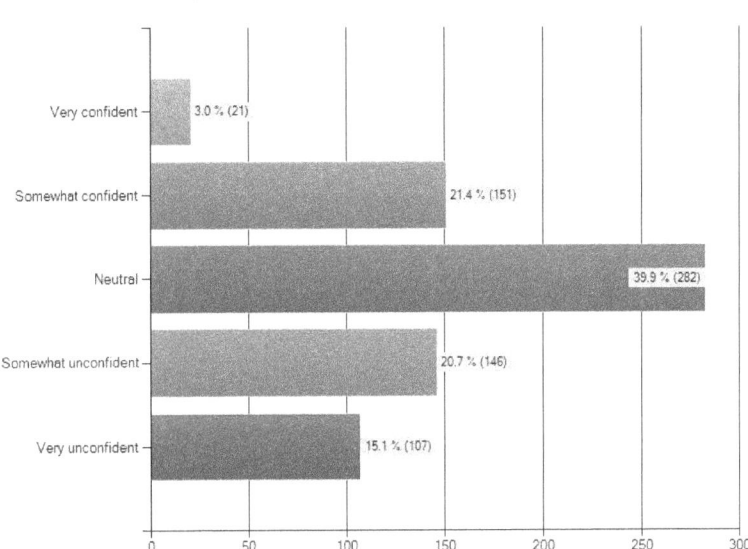

Figure 2: Respondent Confidence in "Natural" Foods' Ability to Reduce Risk of Disease

The mean response to this question is "neutral," and the mode is also "neutral."

Table 5: Respondent Confidence in "Natural" Foods' Ability to Reduce Risk of Disease, Mean Response			
Response	Score	Percent Response	Average (Mean)
Very Confident	5	3.0%	0.15
Somewhat Confident	4	21.4%	0.86
Neutral	3	39.9%	1.20
Somewhat Unconfident	2	20.7%	0.41
Very Unconfident	1	15.1%	0.15
		100.1%	2.77

Finally, when asked whether or not they believed the word "natural" on a front-of-package label has been authorized for use on the label by the U.S. Food and Drug Administration (FDA), 64.8% note they do not believe so, whereas 35.2% believe the FDA does govern the use of this front-of-package label claim.

Table 6: Is "Natural" Authorized by the FDA?		
No	64.8%	458
Yes	35.2%	249

As previously discussed in this article, the FDA has no formal definition of the term "natural," nor does it formally govern its use on front-of-package label claims. Thus, all respondents indicating thoughts that this term was officially governed to mean more than marketing and buzz terminologies could be being misled. This means that the sample's literacy about this particular word as it is used on front-of-package labeling is lacking 35% of the time. Although 35% is a minority portion, it is still a substantive segment of the respondent sample. In the following section, after describing the limitation of my findings, I will provide a discussion of the implications of my findings.

Study Limitations. It should be noted that my study is but one examination of a sample population of consumers. For this study, I utilized convenience sampling at the university where I was employed. While my work yielded a large number of responses, university students may, as a whole, have different interpretations and understandings of front-of-package labels than those surveyed in a general population. However, this work indicates the literacy and interpretations of a sample that can help glean important findings related to a sample's notions about foods labeled as "natural."

Making Meaning of "Natural": Limited Sample Literacies and New FDA Movements

Notes on the Sample Community. While grassroots community campaigns are making aforesaid moves to influence regulatory policies surrounding the word "natural," the results of this survey indicate that, while many members of the sampled community appear literate about some of the apparent issues with "natural" products, a good portion of the community also may not have an understanding about the true "non-definition of 'natural' foods," given the respondents that attributed a specific qualitative meaning to the ingredients and nutritional value of foods labeled as "natural," (see tables 2 and 3). More than 30% of respondents note that they are very confident or somewhat confident: 4.5% of respondents note that they are very confident and 26.4% are somewhat confident. (see figure 1). One quarter of respondents note that they are very confident or somewhat confident that foods labeled as "natural" can actually help prevent disease (see figure 4). Further, more than one third of the respondents do not have an apparent literacy that the word is essentially undefined and not truly regulated by the FDA at this time (see table 6). These findings indicate issues with an overall community literacy of "natural" products and provide a sample of why the "natural" products industry continues to rise, despite lack of regulation in this area.

In a localized look at how "natural" foods may be generally perceived on the UCCS campus itself, and in an attempt to provide context to my findings about the student community's literacy about "natural" foods, a few points are of note: first, UCCS is often regarded as a "green" campus, with its students and the wider campus and area exhibiting a strong knowledge about sustainable and healthy living, which includes, of course, food movements. For example, 2014's Colorado Proposition 105, the failed proposition which would have required stricter mandates on genetically modified foods, including a labeling requirement, was thoroughly covered in an 2014 issue of the *UCCS Scribe*, the university's campus newspaper (Nedd par. 9), with many students chiming in support to the measure. In another 2014 article, a student writer covered the issues of artificial ingredients found in Starbucks lattes. UCCS is home to several informal student clubs, which in the past have indicated a focus on local and natural foods, including the UCCS Local Food Club and the Students for Environmental Awareness and Sustainability. The UCCS Green Action Fund has nearly 300 members on its Facebook group page.

The UCCS community exhibits outward indications of a sustainable campus; the UCCS greenhouse provides organic produce to UCCS's food service locations and offers students a dedicated Office of Sustainability which indicates that providing students with "natural" and "organic" options is a top priority. The campus boasts a very active "Earth Week" campaign annually, with "healthier foods"—whether in the form of local, natural, or organic options—often touted. In 2014, the Princeton Review awarded the UCCS campus distinction as part of the "Green Honor Roll," meaning it earned a place among 24 schools in the nation for sustainable practices, many of which are related to "healthier" and "local, organic foods" (UCCS Office of Sustainability par. 1).

On a larger scale, the local area is seemingly involved in community efforts to fight back against the possible mislabeling of GMO foods as "natural." Colorado Springs is home to one of the annual March Against Monsanto protests. Colorado, as a state, was found to be generally in favor of labeling laws which would alter the state of how many foods labeled as "natural" would be regulated: a *USA Today* poll showed that 51 percent of Coloradans were in favor of the 2014 labeling measure. Colorado's "Right to Know" campaign gained over 170,000 signatures in favor of the effort.

Clearly, the localized environment provides the UCCS student community many opportunities to become informed about issues with foods labeled as "natural," and both UCCS and the city of Colorado Springs, as well as the state of Colorado, maintains an active interest in many of the activist measures described earlier in this article. Yet, the findings of my own survey of the UCCS student community show issues with an overall community literacy of "natural" products; this paradox, in many ways, provides echoes of the idea that there can be a simultaneous community desire to eat "better" or "greener," yet many still choose products that, by many measures, may not actually be so. This echoes the aforementioned bigger picture issue presented by the "American obesity paradox," in which Americans are showing efforts to eat healthier while obesity rates continue to climb.

While the aforementioned grassroots campaigns and lawsuits show progress in gaining community awareness in this area, the movement may not yet be enough, especially considering the continued rise in a community counter movement expressing an approval of "natural" products via the booming "natural" food market and the increasing rate of purchases of these foods. It has been discussed that the FDA recently declined to make further movement on the regulation of the "natural" label, but the organization has made at least some other moves in a proclaimed effort to diminish consumer confusion.

New Movements by the FDA. In early 2014, in an effort to alter elements of food labels the FDA claims are "often misunderstood by consumers," the organization announced changes to the "Nutrition Facts" portion of food labels– changes which would mark the first alteration of this portion of food labels in more than 20 years (FDA 1). Changes that will occur include a bigger emphasis on calories, sugars, and certain nutrients. The "calories from fat" line will be removed, and the daily values for certain nutrients will be updated. Also, the "serving size" portion of the nutrition facts area will receive a makeover—the FDA asserts that the serving size should more accurately reflect the total number of servings so that consumers do not unknowingly consume several servings when they thought the serving size was perhaps just one (FDA 1). While a direct causal effect cannot be noted, this FDA move does chronologically follow several petitions published in 2013, including a major citizen petition by the Center for Science in the Public Interest backed by individuals requesting the addition of an "added sugars" line on the Nutrition Facts panel (CSPI 2). Interestingly enough, the very first change listed in the 2014 FDA proposal would be to "require information about 'added sugars'" (FDA 1).

The question remains as to whether changes regarding the definition and regulation of health claims, particularly those labeled as "natural," will see movement. Perhaps when larger communities exhibit the dissatisfaction made apparent now by those part of the counter literacy about "natural" foods, as evidenced by petitions to the FDA and lawsuits against food companies, the FDA will make this issue a priority. Until then, local communities and grassroots efforts will likely have to push forward to make the issue even more public in order to gain more traction, and research into local community's interpretations and general literacy about foods labeled as "natural" will need to be replicated in an attempt to provide a better overall snapshot of "consumer perceptions and beliefs" (FDA par. 2). While it is questionable as to whether the burden of prompting the FDA to embark on the public process it insists is needed (Kux 2) to formally regulate foods labeled as "natural" should actually lie with consumers (Pomeranz 440), there is also at least some evidence that public community outcry is being noted (Center for Science in the Public Interest 1).

In the context of a nationwide desire and movement to eat healthier, food labels have the potential to be an incredible guiding tool for consumers. Despite all of the nutritional noise surrounding this complex issue, including differing perceptions and limited understandings about regulation of the word "natural," counter community literacies and the subsequent public actions that often form as a result have remarkable potential to inform and grow consumer influence on the food industry. These new literacies and actions, which burst through the surrounding nutritional noise, demonstrate how small community movements can grow into national movements and subsequently begin to change the entire landscape of food labeling.

Works Cited

Center for Science in the Public Interest. Petition to Ensure the Safe Use of "Added Sugars." 13 Feb. 2013. Web. 31 May 2015.

Consumer Reports. "Stop Confusing Consumers: Ban the 'Natural' Label." Takeaction.takepart.com, n.d. Web. 31 May 2015.

Cummins, Ronnie, "Organic Retailers and Consumers Demand Truth in Labeling." Organic Consumers Association. 7 March 3013. Web. 31 May 2015.

Esterl, Mike. "The Natural Evolution of Food Labels." *The Wall Street Journal*, B1. 6 Nov. 2013. Web. 31 May 2015.

Fogel, Stefanie Jill. "FDA declines to define 'Natural'" DLA Piper. 8 Jan. 2014. Web. 31 May 2015.

Food Navigator. "Kampffmeyer asks: What does clean label mean to consumers?" 9 Nov. 2012. Web. 31 May 2015.

Kux, Leslie. "Letter to Judges Gonzalez Rogers, White, and McNulty." 6 Jan. 2014. Web. 31 May 2015.

Nedd, Alexander. GMO Labeling Could Change Food in Colorado. *The UCCS Scribe*. 20 Oct. 2014. Web. 1 Aug. 2015.

Negowetti, Nicole E. "Food Labeling Litigation: Exposing Gaps in the FDA's Resources and Regulatory Authority." Governance Studies At Brookings. June 2014. Web. 31 May 2015.

_____. A National "Natural" Standard for Food Labeling, 65 Me. L. Rev. 581 2013. Web. 31 May 2015.

Pomeranz, Jennifer L. "Litigation To Address Misleading Food Label Claims And The Role Of The State Attorneys." Center for Obesity Research and Education, Temple University. Web. 31 May 2015.

Rangan, Urvashi. "Citizen Petition." Petition to the FDA. 26 June 2014. Web. 31 May 2015.

Sears, William. "Label Loopholes." Ask Dr. Sears. 2015. Web. 31 May 2015.

The Sugar Association. "Citizen Petition." Harris Interactive. 2006. Web. 31 May 2015.

Tierney, John. "Health Halo Can Hide the Calories." *N.Y. Times* 8 Dec. 2008. Web. 31 May 2015.

UCCS Office of Sustainability. UCCS Makes Princeton Review Green Honor Roll! 1 Nov. 2014. Web. 1 Aug. 2015.

U.S. Department of Agriculture's Economic Research Service. "American Adults are Choosing Healthier Foods, Consuming Healthier Diets." 16 Jan. 2014. Web. 31 May 2015.

U.S. Food and Drug Administration. "Proposed Changes to the Nutrition Facts Label." 1 Aug. 2014. Web. 31 May 2015.

———. "What is the meaning of 'natural' on the label of food?" 29 April 2015. Web. 31 May 2015.

Author Bio

Erin Trauth is the Associate Director of Composition and instructor of professional and technical writing at the University of South Florida. She earned her doctorate in Technical Communication and Rhetoric at Texas Tech University. She conducts research on front-of-package food labels and regulatory policies surrounding this communication, public health communication, risk communication, service learning, writing for non-profit organizations, composition pedagogy, and computer-mediated communications.

De aquí y de allá: Changing Perceptions of Literacy through Food Pedagogy, Asset-Based Narratives, and Hybrid Spaces

Lucía Durá, Consuelo Salas, William Medina-Jerez, and Virginia Hill

In this article we describe La Escuelita Afterschool Program, an interdisciplinary, inter-institutional, after-school literacy partnership on the U.S.–Mexico border. The Escuelita Program used food pedagogy to tap into funds of knowledge, bridging home and school literacies. In doing so, the program challenged deficit thinking and enhanced K-6 students' curiosity and engagement around traditional subjects: science, math, reading, and writing. Through a process of experimental curriculum design and a variety of qualitative data collection methods, we discuss how food pedagogy can help to change deficit-based narratives and how it helps expand the scope of literacy acquisition.

Antes de venir a la escuelita sí sabía mucho de maíz pero no se me ocurrió platicarle a mis hijas. Cuando ya vinimos a la Escuelita y que ya era el tema de ese año, y mis hijas me preguntaron "Mami tu sabías de esa planta?" Sí, y por qué no nos habías dicho? Y sabías de esto y esto? Pues sí pero estamos esperando que fuéramos al rancho. Ya ellas empezaron a conocer todo sobre del maíz y que consumimos y que no sabíamos, no sabían que es tan importante sobre el maíz.

Before coming to the Escuelita I did know a great deal about corn but I did not think to share that with my daughters. When we began coming to the Escuelita I discovered that was the subject of the year, and my daughters asked me "Mami you knew of this plant?" [I responded] Yes, and [my daughters asked] why didn't you tell us? And [they asked] you knew about this and this? [I responded] Well yes, but I was waiting to go to the ranch. They began learning all about the corn we eat, things we didn't know and why it is so important.

—"Alicia," La Escuelita Afterschool Program Parent

Our city, situated on the U.S.–Mexico border, ranks consistently low in well-known studies of literacy (Miller). These studies focus on traditional definitions and markers of literacy such as number of bookstores, average educational attainment, and availability of periodical publishing resources. Yet, as we know, literacy is highly complex and involves the intersection of countless internal and external factors. Studies like Miller's decide whose culture has capital, and, in doing so, fuel public perception of literacy deficiencies (Yosso). They exclude more nuanced markers of literacy like bilingualism and biculturalism as proposed in *Generaciones' Narratives* by John Scenters-Zápico. Even when speaking more than one language and being fluent in more than one culture are common, necessary, and valued, as is the case in our location, conversations about literacy focus largely on deficits (Sepúlveda). This is problematic because *global* perceptions of literacy feed into *local* classroom practices, and these classroom practices, in turn, reinforce a learning culture—one that influences what we think we are capable of or destined to accomplish (Engberg and Allen), i.e., the stories we tell ourselves about ourselves (Geertz).

As educator Luis Moll argues, "existing classroom practices underestimate and constrain what Latino and other children are able to display intellectually" (179). Through his concept of Funds of Knowledge, Moll advocates turning to asset-based learning, especially in communities where such assets might be hidden from plain view. "Alicia's" quote at the beginning of this article, originally in Spanish and translated into English, is illustrative of the types of food and literacy connections the Escuelita Program facilitated. In this article we propose food pedagogy as an effective medium to tap into Funds of Knowledge. We describe "La Escuelita Afterschool Program," (Escuelita Program) an interdisciplinary, inter-institutional, after-school literacy partnership in El Paso, Texas.[1] The Escuelita Program used a food pedagogy-based curriculum to challenge deficit thinking and boost K-6 students' curiosity and engagement around traditional subjects: science, math, reading, and writing.

In the sections that follow we explain our theoretical and conceptual perspectives, contextualize our project and study, and answer the following research questions: (1) How does food pedagogy tap into funds of knowledge? (2) How does making connections between "home" and "school" knowledge challenge deficit-based perceptions of literacies? We conclude with a brief discussion of implications and areas for future research.

Our Theoretical and Conceptual Perspectives

Funds of Knowledge

Some areas of academia are beginning to move away from the ideology that knowledge is only created within the classroom space. This transition allows what is generally regarded as untraditional or "home knowledge" to hold as much cultural capital as school knowledge. Moll and other scholars refer to this as Funds of Knowledge (FoK), "knowledge of strategic importance to households" (Moll and Greenberg 323). FoK includes knowledge about farming, medicinal remedies, and home or auto repair, but also institutional access, school programs, and occupational opportunities. FoK "[contrasts] sharply with prevailing and accepted perceptions of working class families as somehow disorganized socially and deficient intellectually" (Moll, Amanti, Neff, and Gonzalez, 134). Re-examining what counts as knowledge opens a space where minority students are seen not as deficient in traditional conceptions of knowledge or literacy, but instead rich in other FoK and literate in other contexts. As argued by Moll et al., "by capitalizing on household and other community resources, we can organize classroom instruction that far exceeds in quality the rote-like instruction these children commonly encounter in schools" (132). Several studies hold FoK at their core for re-examining teacher preparation; they advocate for teachers to recognize, examine, acknowledge, and leverage the FoK with which their students enter the classroom (See Licona; Calabrese Barton, and Tan; Vélez-Ibáñez and Greenberg; Moll and Greenberg; Moll, Amanti, Neff, Gónzalez).

Asset-Based Community Work and Hybrid Spaces

The concept of FoK dovetails well with asset-based thinking in community work in rhetoric and composition (RC). Asset-based thinking "begins with assets instead of deficits" (Grabill 96). It encourages an ideological stance that gives people agency and credit for their current expertise; positions community members as co-constructors of knowledge, not merely as "clients" in need of a service provided by outsiders (Grabill 96); and encourages active participation instead of passive reception (See Cushman; Grabill; Mathieu; Simmons; Flower; and Long). Although FoK focus on assets and are seen as a desirable pedagogical practice, it is also important to note that enacting such pedagogy in a traditional classroom may be difficult, even more so in an environment of high stakes standardized testing. Science education scholar Miguel Licona argues that a "FoK approach requires teachers to become ethnographers" (869). The extra time educators must take to visit their students' homes and learn their FoK may be asking too much of our teachers.

Several scholars, however, have studied how "hybrid spaces," such as community centers, can be ideal places to reveal and capitalize on students' FoK (See Buxton; Seiler). In their study merging FoK, discourses, and hybrid space in science education, Angela Calabrese Barton and Edna Tan explain the value of hybridity:

> We are interested in notions of hybridity because we have observed how youth take up knowledges, resources, and identities that often go unsanctioned in school. In so doing, they author new identities, drawing from nontraditional funds and Discourses [sic] to renegotiate the boundaries of their participation in class in ways that allow them to build their social identities while establishing epistemic authority. (52, 53)

Hybrid spaces facilitate "meeting halfway" and certain neutrality that allows for non-threatening conversation and shared decision-making. Yet, in addition to finding the right physical space, rhetorical framing is crucial for setting a tone of invitation and co-ownership. Otherwise, how does an "outsider" get an invitation to "help"? In our particular project, we anchored engagement in food.

Food Pedagogy

When we discuss, "food pedagogy" we speak of it from a Food Studies perspective. According to food scholar Warren Belasco,

> […] "food extends far beyond nutrients, calories, and minerals." A meal is much more than the sum of its parts, for it encompasses what Barthes calls "a system of communication, a body of images, a protocol of usages, situations, and behavior." […] People use food to "speak" with each other, to establish rules of behavior ("protocols"), and to reveal as Brillat-Savarin said, "what you are." (15)

Food studies is a multidisciplinary, multifaceted discipline that examines the diverse aspects of *food*, from gender, race, class, to psychology, philosophy, consumption, production and distribution (See Counihan and van Esterik). In our use of "food pedagogy," food is an "object, site, target and 'technology' of education and learning" and is a "*vehicle* for learning" (emphasis in the original, Flowers and Swan 419, 423). "Food pedagogy" is "a congeries of education, teaching and learning about how to grow shop for, prepare, cook display, taste, eat and dispose of food by a range of agencies, actors and media; and aimed [at] a spectrum of 'learners' … " (426). All of these activities are packed with tacit knowledge, and by making such everyday knowledge explicit, we have the opportunity to make explicit both traditional literacies, typically learned in books or school, and FoK. We propose that food pedagogy has great rhetorical weight as an entry point to engaging community literacies. Scholars and practitioners in the field of education have found creative ways to elicit FoK, and we believe that by putting the work that is being done in education, RC, food studies and food pedagogy in conversation will allow more fruitful harvests of information about the groups we work with.

Our Partnership

How We Came to Be

Our Escuelita Program team is part of an interdisciplinary research group formed in 2011 at The University of Texas at El Paso (UTEP). The mission of this group has been to develop, implement, and document integrated intervention programs that contribute to health and educational equity among Hispanic populations, particularly through translational research. The Escuelita Program is a spin-off of this group. During initial meetings, which took place at the UTEP library, notions of literacy, STEM, culture, and cooking surfaced, and curiosity solidified around the following questions:

- How is it that in bilingual communities like ours conversations focus so much on deficits?

- What would happen if we re-wrote the script of our literacy story? How might we see traditional literacies (science, math, reading, and writing) through a cultural lens?

- Might we see changes in the ways our students perceive themselves? Might we see changes in the ways students are perceived by others? Might we see changes in students' educational outcomes?

The team grew to include faculty and graduate students in science education, RC, literature, food studies and art; resident relations specialists from the Housing Authority of the City of El Paso (HACEP); teachers and aides from a local school district; and students in grades K-6 and their parents. Our common interdisciplinary and inter-institutional denominator? Food. We decided to use food pedagogy to anchor lessons, hands-on cooking, and conversations about ourselves and our heritage.

Our ultimate goal was to write and test a curriculum specifically for after-school programs that used food as a "hook" for students to engage traditionally challenging concepts or subjects. The pilot project (which we also to refer to as Year 1) was titled "The HACEP-UTEP After-school Pilot Project: Promoting Scientific and Literacy Skills through Culture-based Activities." It came to be known informally as the Escuelita Program (*escuelita* is a diminutive, and endearing, term for school in Spanish). The project in Year 2 was titled "Using Corn to Bridge Home and School Literacies: A Culture-based, After-school Curriculum Merging Science, Math, Geography, History, Reading, and Writing."

HACEP and The Escuelitas. HACEP manages 6,500 public residential units comprising multi-family, scattered sites, and elderly communities, which represent 40,000 residents whose average annual income is below $10,000. According to Holly Mata et al., single females with children comprise over fifty percent of HACEP households. Almost half of HACEP residents are under the age of 14. HACEP residents are predominately of Hispanic heritage (98%) and mostly Mexican immigrants and Mexican-Americans.

HACEP hosts four Escuelita sites. Escuelitas are both programs and physical spaces (usually one room with access to the larger community center) contained in the different HACEP community centers throughout the city. A teacher and several tutors or aides from one of the local school districts work with students from that community after school. Among the school district and HACEP communities, Escuelitas are generally perceived as places where students receive tutoring and enrichment activities or do homework.

Educational Partners and Curriculum Overview. The two institutional educational partners for this project were UTEP and a local school district.[2] Collaborating partners from these institutions included

> **William Medina-Jerez**—PI of the Escuelita Program. He is originally from Colombia and is an Associate Professor in Science Education. He worked with three cohorts of pre-service elementary teachers in science education as part of the project.

Lucía Durá—Co-PI for the project. She is an Assistant Professor in RC with a background in participatory action research, language, food writing, and food pedagogy.

Consuelo Salas—Ph.D. student in RC with a background in Food Studies. She designed and implemented sessions with Dr. FS on food and culture. She conducted ethnographic research using Activity Theory during the project and provided observational feedback for the collaborating team.

Francisco Valente Saénz—M.A. art student who worked on a separate collaborative, public art project with HA residents. He introduced Drs. Medina-Jerez and Durá.

Meredith Abarca—Associate Professor of English Literature and a Food Studies scholar. She implemented one session in Year 1 and helped to co-design and implement the curriculum in Year 2. She brought a Food Studies and culture lens to the project.

Virginia Hill and Sonia Legarreta—two resident relations specialists from HACEP, who link residents with services that can improve quality of life.

Ms. GB—Escuelita teacher for Year 1. She worked diligently with the students in between formal Escuelita sessions on vocabulary-building and reading and writing.

Ms. IH—an art teacher from Ms. GB's school who documented our work using photography and video and facilitated use of the school's computer lab when needed for art projects.

Ms. ML—Escuelita teacher for Year 2. She was instrumental in helping us design age-appropriate activities. Her daughter was also an Escuelita participant.

Ms. JS—school district Specialist and official partnership liaison.

School district tutors—two to three tutors from the school district supported the work of the Escuelita students and teachers. They did not participate in planning sessions but were present at feedback/research sessions.

Methodology

Curriculum Development as a Design Experiment

Inspired by Calabrese Barton and Tan's science education study on "Funds of Knowledge and Discourses and Hybrid Space," we approached our work of curriculum development as a design experiment. A design experiment in educational research, as explained by Cobb, Confrey, diSessa, Lehrer, Schauble, is meant "to develop a class of theories about both the process of learning and the means that are designed to support that learning" (10). Design experiments are necessarily (1) praxis-based, (2) interventionist, (3) prospective—based on a hypothesis, (4) iterative, and (5) immediately relevant to practitioners, i.e., resulting theories are pragmatic (Cobb et al. 9-11). In a way similar to Calabrese and Tan, we used our design experiment to address simultaneously problems of practice and develop/test principles of teaching and learning that might be applicable beyond the original research site.

Data Collection and Analysis

Given the speculative and iterative nature of conducting a design experiment, we drew from a variety of data collection methods to reflect on the process and products and feed insights back into project design over the course of each school year. In Year 1, we collected data anchored in food-based lessons. This included artifacts (e.g., drawings, writing, and photographs/video), narratives (oral and written), and observations (several of us kept research journals). We also conducted focus groups with family members and interviewed children participants. In addition to these methods, in Year 2 we added an Activity Theory ethnography, which Consuelo conducted for a methods course in her doctoral program, and asset-based, participatory methods: Appreciative Interviews (AIs) (Lipmanowicz & McCandless), Cultural Memory Banking (CMB) (Handa & Tippins), Participatory Interviews, and Participatory Drawing and Narrations. We analyzed all data continuously as a team using Glaser & Strauss' constant comparative method to extract key themes. We also employed visual discourse analysis to interpret the composition, context, and reception of images (See Christmann and Durá et al.).

Curriculum Design and Implementation

Our first research question asks, how does food pedagogy tap into funds of knowledge? To answer this question, in this section we describe key insights from the recursive curriculum design and implementation process. In the mode of Jessica Seinfeld who writes healthy recipes under the auspices of "yummy" foods, in Year 1 we set out to write a curriculum for the Escuelita Program that used food to "grab" students' attention so that they may explore science, math, reading, and writing along the way. We also aimed to re-write the script of our literacy story by viewing traditional school literacies through a cultural lens.

We used food to anchor all lessons, invited parents to participate often, incorporated art as much as possible, and coordinated lessons with the seasons or holidays, e.g., planting time, harvest time, Thanksgiving, etc. (Gónzalez and Moll). Each session contained one or more 90-minute lesson. The curriculum sequence we followed in Years 1 and 2 is in table 1.

Table 1. Curriculum Sequence for Year 1 and Year 2 Design Experiment

YEAR 1	YEAR 2
	Preliminary Session with Families: "Appreciative Interviews" (AIs) and "Cultural Memory Bank" (CMB). Escuelita Program team brings home cooked meal to share with parents.
Session 1: *"The Favorite Plate"* Ms. CG, guides students in the design of a colorful plate representing their favorite meal using the 5 Ws as a heuristic.	**Session 1:** *"Where does corn come from?"* Incorporates history and geography in tracing the historical migration of corn from different areas of the world to the students' plates. Writing activity: map and corn diagram with various species (i.e., yellow, blue, hominy, Peruvian) and their descriptions.
Session 2: *"Practicing with Cooking Techniques"* Prior to this session Ms. CG prepares a glossary of the terms students practice using. Students perform different cooking techniques, e.g., measuring, mixing, and folding. They prepare *calabacitas* (Mexican squash side dish), *merengues* (meringues), and *melcochas* (Colombian caramels) with guidance and are introduced to food science.	**Session 2:** *"What food is made with corn?"* Incorporates cultural history and nutrition in making direct connections with familiar recipes. Recipe reading and writing activities using visual-to-written templates (See fig. 1).
Session 3: *"Cooking with Families."* Students read bilingual books: *Adelita and the Veggie Cousins/ Adelita y las primas verduritas* and *A Day without Sugar/Un día sin azúcar*. Each family brings a vegetable and/or a fruit to be used in preparation of a soup and fruit skewers. Students and their parents practice the cooking techniques and write a family recipe (using a template) that uses at least one fruit and/or vegetable.	**Session 3:** *"Who makes foods made with corn?"* Incorporates cultural history in greater depth, including family history. Uses a cultural artifact exhibit as teachers provided a *metate* (stone grinder), hand *molino* (mill), tortilla press, and *comal* (hot plate) to demonstrate culturally significant traditional ways of processing corn in the home. Students interview a family member or neighbor using a template to record responses. They also bring a corn "artifact" and write a short story about it.

Year 1	Year 2
	Interim Session with Families: Videotaped family member interviews and potluck.
Session 4: *"Revising Recipes."* Students go through a peer review process of their family recipes and revise with help of tutors. Students write a recipe for cold sandwich wraps using a visual-to-writing template (See fig. 1).	Session 4: *"What other things are made with corn?"* Teachers demonstrate the multiple uses of corn. Demonstration of physical objects that are also made with corn; for example, batteries, etc. Students not only have the opportunity to write, but physically see how science uses food for purposes outside of nutrition.
Session 5: *"The Ideal/Colorful Plate."* Introduction of the USDA/Harvard/Michelle Obama plate for comparison with the students' initial plate. Students color the "Obama" plate and work on a third plate: their "improved" favorite plate, which they explain.	Session 5: *"Why is corn important?"* Students reflect on the information they have learned throughout the unit, and considered the various cultural, historical, and scientific implications of corn. In a group writing exercise or through picture books students compose a story of why they believe corn is important.
Sessions 6 and 7: *"The Faces of Food."* In Part I, students use bagels and vegetables to represent a family member's face. They tell an oral story about the person. In Part II, students use ingredients for Mexican tostadas to create a face that expresses how they feel that day. They describe their face and that particular emotion(s).	
Culminating Event with Families: Students and their families received a compilation of the Escuelita recipes, including Escuelita and family recipes.	Culminating Event with Families: Stories are compiled, formatted into an illustrated book/booklet, and presented to the wider housing, school district, and university community.

Year 1 Insights

At the end of Year 1 our team learned four key lessons. First, constant with the process of design experiments as a methodology, the curriculum was under constant revision. For example, we added Sessions 6 as a result of Meredith and Consuelo joining the team. Meredith had done the bagel face activity in a different setting and introduced us to it. We then added the tostada face—Session 7—for cultural relevance as we learned that some students were unfamiliar with bagels. Second, we found that some of the most successful moments involved family members cooking with students and family members sharing recipes. Recipes are a conversation starter, even within family units. For example, students had questions for their parents about the techniques and the origins of the recipes. Third, we learned that positioning students as makers and doers brings out other ways of knowing. This ontological dimension is a valuable aspect of food pedagogy. Making or cooking allows students to work with their hands and learn something about themselves. It also enables them to "know" what they are describing in oral or written form. Students felt that if they lacked the vocabulary for something, "showing" was a valid technique. Art as "doing" worked in a similar way. Using a visual to written template, students draw the steps in a recipe first and then describe the steps in words (See fig. 1 below). This meets students where they are and allows all of them to be active participants, regardless of skill level.

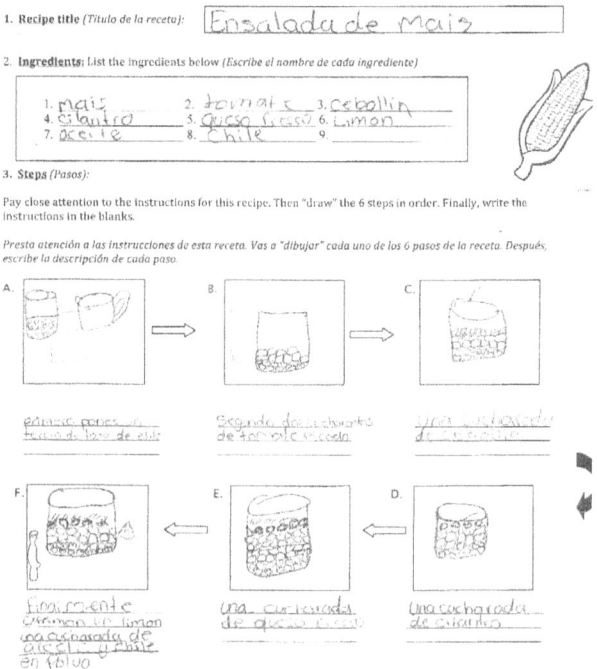

Figure. 1. Visual to Written Recipe Template

A fourth lesson is leveraging the richness of our linguistic backgrounds, e.g., hybridity. When students had the ability to choose a language for a particular activity, they didn't feel "stuck." And yet, the curricular structure gave them plenty of opportunities to also practice their more challenging language.

Year 2 Insights

Based on what we learned in Year 1, in Year 2 we began the program with a greater emphasis on participatory and asset-based techniques. We decided to focus on an agricultural theme that would be relevant for everyone involved—something that everyone had access to, that was in our daily diets, and that grows in the area. We chose corn. And seeing the value of family narratives in Year 1, we decided to incorporate appreciative interviews and cultural memory banking from the first session. AIs are meant to discover and build on the root causes of success—as opposed to failure or barriers (Lipmanowicz & McCandless). Using AIs, questions are structured for positive discovery and storytelling, e.g., think back to when you were growing up, what was your favorite food? Who would make it? What do you remember about the tastes, ingredients? When would you eat it? Where? We used this question sequence in our first session with families to begin to populate our CMB. We used a CMB to "store" all of our findings from interviews, focus groups, observations, field trips, and lessons. This CMB was displayed on the walls of the Escuelita site and was available for all participants to populate with words, sentences, and images. Field trips during Year 2 included visits to local food factories, grocery stores, and a local corn maze; they were planned to help reinforce lessons within the class time.

At the end of Year 2, in the summer, our team met to compile lessons into a written curriculum for replication. We analyzed the findings from both years, and we structured the curriculum document as a recipe in which we explained these findings as "Essential Ingredients." Our instructions for the users read:

> We have framed this thematic unit as a recipe—not one to be followed to the letter, but one to be adapted to your needs. Some ingredients, we have found, are essential. They are what helps create bridges between home and school. Others are more flexible. Their quantities can be tweaked a bit more. In this section we describe the key ingredients for the unit. *¡Buen provecho!* Enjoy! (Medina-Jerez, Durá, & López)

The essential ingredients we describe in the curriculum are

- Food pedagogy not only helps to "break the ice" in any group, it also helps to tap into students' "Funds of Knowledge" and empowers students in the "doing." Students are able to learn *about* food as the topic engages a wide variety of people, but they are also able to learn *through* food: "food can be a useful teaching tool to develop an understanding of science and math concepts" (Phillips, Duffrin & Geist 24).

- A hybrid space (after-school) provided opportunities for creativity without the pressure of state assessments (tests and standards). It also provided opportunities for family members to attend and to talk to each other.

- A locally important food theme that lends itself to conversations about heritage and that is infinitely "explorable" serves as a good point of departure for inquiry. We found an agricultural theme to be relevant. Other locations might choose a theme that is relevant for other reasons, i.e., geography, industry, history.

- Family involvement grounds the FoK discovery process in heritage and home practices. It also maximizes the likelihood that ideas children bring home will be adopted/sustained.

- Inquiry structure—framing this as an exploration helps us all learn together instead of the educators as teachers and the participants as learners.

- Art, hands-on activities, field-trips and guest teachers, in ways similar to food, position students as makers and doers, creating a space for physical meaning-making, increased-self awareness, and different perspectives/new narratives.

- Explicit "transfer" language helps participants make connections about knowledge and ways of knowing from one sphere to the other.

Aligning the Classroom and Kitchen Spaces: Threads from Participants

In order to answer our second question—how does making connections between "home" and "school" knowledge challenge deficit-based perceptions of literacies?—we first describe the three part process of using "*charlas culinarias*" to make connections. We then present insights, which we have grouped thematically using a constant comparative method (Glaser & Strauss), from data collected from students, parents, and teachers over the course of Years 1 and 2 of the Escuelita Program.

Making Connections through *Charlas Culinarias*

If indeed our realities are shaped by language—by the stories we tell ourselves—then changing those stories becomes crucial in order to challenge deficit-based perceptions. Abarca explains that *charlas culinarias* "[…] represent spoken personal narratives, testimonial autobiography, and a form of culinary memoir […] (166). In the Escuelita Program, we worked to create an environment that asked parents of student participants to speak to their culinary FoK within the hybrid space of a classroom and community center. Eliciting these stories through *charlas* was a first step towards making connections between home and school. We did this in a couple of ways: (1) recipe sharing and cooking together in Year 1, and (2) integrating AIs, Participatory Interviews, and the CMB in Year 2. Through our *charlas* we attempted to move through three steps:

- Step 1: Inviting the parents to share their stories about food, production, and consumption both with their children and with other families and creating a space where those stories are cherished and valued;

- Step 2: Fostering an environment that allowed families to recognize their food production, consumption, and distribution knowledge as a literacy, i.e., knowledge that perhaps they had never before considered to be a literacy but simply a means of providing for their families;

- Step 3: In going through steps 1 and 2 with the parents, we used food to tap into students' funds of knowledge and (1) create a sense that what occurs in the kitchen is a valuable literacy; 2) make explicit connections to multiple subjects, science, geography, reading, writing, history, and using food to expand students' notions of those subjects.

Cooking as a Scientific Process

At the onset of Year 2, we conducted AIs with parents. This *charla* took place with families around a simple question: "What foods do you eat or make that have corn?" We asked parents to speak in pairs, then in fours, and then shared with the whole group stories about their cultural cooking practices as well as who they were, where they were from, and a bit about their family history. The parents explained that never before had they considered that their caloric funds of knowledge or food preparation, could be scientific; however, in the AIs parents described, for example, that they had knowledge of how to start a fire without the use of the stove—using firewood outside. Once the fire was lit, they then had the know how to keep the flame at the right temperature to prepare the foods. Parents, especially mothers, also had knowledge of various recipes involving the *nixtamalización* process (soaking corn in lime and boiling it to facilitate grinding and enhance the *masa's* (corn dough) nutritional value), different types of corn for different uses, and different tools that were used to process the corn such as the *metate* (stone grinder) for grinding and the *comal* (hot plate) for cooking. We "stored" this knowledge in the CMB.

Valuing Food Literacies

Midway through Year 2, we held a potluck to which parents brought their favorite recipes made with corn. The students conducted Participatory Interviews. They followed an interview format and were videotaped asking their parents questions about their favorite dishes and recipes made with corn. It is worth noting that, in large part, parents were not shy in front of the camera. Rather, they were enthusiastic to share more stories, and they asserted that they were very happy to share food with us as we had done with them. Thus the tone for the session was generous and festive.

Through the *charlas*, parents were able to take on an authoritative role in their FoK as preparers of food. One working parent talked about the importance of *sazón*. In her interview she explained why one should make food taste good: "Es importante tener buena sazón. Si a la gente le gusta la comida le van a preguntar a uno como la hizo y le van a pedir más." For this parent, good tasting food was a commodity. She said that if food tasted good people would want to know how it was made, and in a financial pinch, one could sell it. She further explained that she felt equipped to sell food if she ever lost her job. Other parents talked about the importance of passing down their heritage through food—mostly to their daughters; although one parent said she would also pass it to her son. At the end of Year 2, we conducted participatory drawing activities with parents, asking them to depict signs of change "before" and "after" engaging in the Escuelita Program. "I had never given importance to where food comes from," said one parent. "Now when we're eating, we have these conversations." Another parent talked about valuing her roots and explained that when they go to the ranch in the future her children want to help warm the tortillas and learn about more things you can do with corn: "El rancho es un vil rancho, de adobe. [Ellos] no quieren salir de la cocina, donde se hacen las tortillas. Pero cuantas cosas se hacían con el maíz? [Y]o, conocía muy poquito." A parent added that her daughter now wants to discuss similarities and differences with other Latin cultures.

Students as Makers and Doers

Cooking activities in the Escuelita Program were designed to support the translation of everyday practices into authentic learning opportunities to practice scientific habits of mind that include predicting, calculating, observing, and inferring, among others. While engaged in the cooking activities, students were able to practice reading and writing skills included in the planning, preparation, and presentation of each recipe and activity (e.g., follow directions, summarization, compare and contrast) both in Spanish and in English. A prevalent theme for both years of the Escuelita Program was that student participants stayed active and engaged with the projects both within the Escuelita setting and at home in the kitchen space. In the end-of-year focus groups, students spoke about which activities they remembered most or found to be their favorites. Students from Year 1 (even at the end of Year 2 when we conducted follow-up interviews) remembered the activities that involved cooking: making soup, fruit skewers, and *merengues* and *melcochas*. Students from Year 2 remembered tortillas to make *quesadillas*, visiting the grocery store and reading food labels, making a colorful corn salad, and doing a silk-screen painting of their favorite take-aways from the year with a narration. Similarly, when we asked students about the differences they saw between the work they do at the Escuelita and the work they do in their regular classrooms, students from both years pointed to the "doing." "Here we are working together," one student said. "Here we do activities. At school we do more worksheets," another student said.

In their before/after drawings and narrations parents from Year 1 noted that their children do tasks such as help wash vegetables, chop vegetables, and read the ingredient labels. They also say things like, "I am a chef" or "this ingredient tastes good with this other one." In explaining before/after changes at the end of Year 1, Ms. GB said that while most of the Escuelita participants were not in her class at school, they would very proudly say hello to her in the hallway. To her this was significant as she explained that students from lower grades (she teaches 6th grade) do not customarily speak to or reach out to teachers from higher grades, much less publicly.

In the case of students from Year 2, they read food labels and tell their parents when corn is an unexpected ingredient, such as with hamburger buns or ketchup. Students from Year 2 also replicate easy recipes such as the corn salad with their parents. Ms. ML noted the significance of this theme: "Before, students were just observers. They would watch their parents. Now they do things. They can do things that they watched others do, and that's empowering!" She also added that this curriculum is similar to what students in "Gifted and Talented" classes get, and this population is not typically exposed to such programming. Virginia and Sonia also observed that students stayed excited and were more engaged throughout the year with our involvement; they noted that students transferred some ideas from the cooking sessions to the garden project in their residential community.

Conclusion: *De aquí y de allá*

The saying, "Ni de aquí, ni de allá" in Spanish means "from neither here nor there." It refers to the immigrant's conundrum of physical and metaphorical liminality. Our title, *De aquí y de allá*, is a both/and proposition. The work presented in this article challenges deficit-based perceptions by bridging home and school literacies. It encourages a both/and perspective instead of either/or. Through the Escuelita Program we have described how food pedagogy taps into family FoK. Honoring and bearing witness to FoK laid the groundwork for a learning environment that encouraged students to engage in what they were are already familiar with, value it, see it as a literacy, and use it to learn other subjects. Food pedagogy, in tapping into funds of knowledge, helps to expand the scope of literacy acquisition by changing the narrative about what people can expect from themselves. And learning by doing builds the confidence and know-how to transfer literacies (broadly speaking) or skills from one space to another. It is through this framework that communities traditionally seen as illiterate can begin to expand and question traditional notions of literacy.

There is great potential in food-literacy partnerships, and this is just the beginning. As food continues to trend, so can explorations and experiments with food pedagogy. Many aspects of this project can be investigated further, e.g., reading and writing artifacts, learning STEM subjects through food, the epistemological and ontological dimensions of food pedagogy, and the relationship between food pedagogy and learning outcomes. We encourage other scholars and practitioners to apply the Escuelita model of community engagement with their local communities in a way that makes sense to their context. And we welcome conversations that further inquiry as we continue to explore the Escuelita Program's curriculum replication.

Endnotes

1. The Escuelita project was funded by The University of Texas at El Paso's College of Education Research Grants for Associate Professors program. We are thankful for this financial support. We also thank Meredith Abarca for her influence in the design, facilitation, and documentation of this work; for guiding us into the field of Food Studies; and for reviewing this manuscript. We are indebted to all Escuelita students and families and to our collaborating partners Sonia Legarreta, Francisco Valente Saenz, Ms. IH, Ms. GB, Ms. ML, and Ms. JS. This work would not be possible without their participation and feedback.

2. In accordance with our confidentiality agreements, we are using pseudonyms for school district partner names.

Works Cited

Abarca, Meredith E. *Voices in the Kitchen: Views of Food and the World from Working Class Mexican and Mexican American Women*. College Station: Texas A&M Press, 2006. Print.

Belasco, Warren. *Food: The Key Concepts*. New York: Berg, 2008. Print.

Buxton, Cory. "Creating contextually authentic science in a low performing urban elementary school. *Journal of Research in Science Teaching* 43.7 (2006) : 695–721.

Calabrese Barton, Angela and Edna Tan. "Funds of Knowledge and Discourses in Hybrid Space." *Journal of Research in Science Teaching* 46.1 (2009) : 50-73. Print.

Calabrese Barton, Angela, Toby J. Hindin, Isobel R. Contento, Michelle Trudeau, Kimberley Yang, Sumi Hagiwara, and Pamela Koch. "Underprivileged Urban Mothers' Perspective on Science." *Journal of Research in Science Teaching* 38.6 (2001) : 688-711. Print.

Carlton Parsons, Eileen and Heidi B. Carlone. "Culture and science Education in the 21st century: Extending and making the cultural box more inclusive." *Journal of Research in Science Teaching* 50.1 (2012) : 1-11. Web. 28 May 2015 doi: 10.1002tea.21068

Christmann, Gabriela B. "The Power of Photographs of Buildings in the Dresden Urban Discourse. Towards a Visual Discourse Analysis." *Forum: Qualitative Social Research Sozialforschung* 9.3 (2008) : np. Web. 28 May 2015.

Cobb, Paul, Jere Confrey, Andrea diSessa, Richard Lehrer, and Leona Schauble. "Design Experiments in Educational Research." *Educational Researcher* 32.1 (2003) : 9-13. Print.

Counihan, Carole and Penny Van Esterik. "Why Food? Why Culture? Why Now? Introduction to the Third Edition." *Food and Culture: A Reader*. 3d ed. Eds. Carole Counihan and Penny Van Esterik. Routledge: New York, 2013. Print.

Cushman, Ellen. *The struggle and the tools: Oral and literate strategies in an inner city community*. Albany: SUNY Press, 1998. Print.

Durá, Lucía, Laurel J. Felt, and Arvind Singhal. "What Counts? For Whom? Cultural Beacons and Unexpected Areas of Programmatic Impact." *Journal of Evaluation and Program Planning*, 44 (2014) : 98-109. Print.

Edbauer Rice, Jenny and Jeff Rice. *Pre/Text: A Journal of Rhetorical Theory Food Theory*. 21.1-4 (2013). Print.

Engberg, Mark E. and Daniel J. Allen. "Uncontrolled destinies: Improving opportunity for low income students in American higher education." *Research in Higher Education* 52.8 (2011) : 786-807. Web. 18 May 2015

Flower, Linda. *Community Literacy and the Rhetoric of Public Engagement*. Carbondale: Southern Illinois UP, 2008. Print.

Flowers, Rick and Elaine Swan. "Introduction: Why food? Why pedagogy? Why adult education?" *Australian Journal of Adult Learning*. 52.3 (2012) : 419-430. Print.

Frye, Joshua and Michael Bruner. *Rhetoric of Food*. New York: Routledge, 2012. Print.

Geertz, Clifford. *The Interpretation of Culture: Selected Essays*. New York: Basic Books, 1973. Print.

Grabill, Jeffrey T. *Community Literacy Program and the Politics of Change*. New York: SUNY Press, 2001. Print.

Glaser, Barney and Anselm Strauss. *The Discovery of Grounded Theory: Strategies for Qualitative Research* New Brunswick: Aldine Transaction, 1967; 2012. Print.

González, Norma E, & Moll, Luis. "Cruzando el puente: Building bridges to funds of knowledge." *Journal of Educational Policy*, 16.4 (2002) : 623-641. Print.

Hagiwara, Sumi, Angela Calabrese-Barton, and Isobel R. Contento. "Culture, food, and language: Perspectives from immigrant mothers in school science." *Cultural Studies of Science Education*, 2 (2007) : 475-499. Print.

Handa, Vicente C. and Deborah J. Tippins. "Cultural Memory Banking in Preservice Science Teacher Education." *Research Science Education*. 42.6(2012): 1201-1217. Print. doi:10.1007/s11165-011-9241-6

Licona, Miguel M. "Mexican and Mexican-American children's funds of knowledge as interventions into deficit thinking: opportunities for praxis in science education." *Culture Studies of Science Education* 8 (2013) : 859-872. Doi 10.1007/s11422- 0139515-6. Print.

Lipmanowicz, Henri and Keith McCandless. "Appreciative Interviews." *Liberating Structures: Innovating by Including and Unleashing Everyone. E&Y Performance* 2.4 (2010) : 6-9. Web 30 May 2015.

Long, Eleanore. *Community Literacy and the Rhetoric of Local Publics* West Lafayette: Parlor Press, 2008. Electronic.

Mata, Holly, Maria Flores, Ernesto Castañeda, William Medina-Jerez, Josue Lachica, Curtis Smith, and Hector Olvera. "Health, hope, and human development: Building capacity in public housing communities on the U.S.–Mexico border." *Journal of Health Care for the Poor and Underserved* 24.4(2013) : 1432-1439.

Matheiu, P. *Tactics of hope: The public turn in English composition*. Portsmouth, NH: Boynton/Cook, 2005. Print.

Medina-Jerez William, Lucía Durá and Marisela Lopez. "Bridging Home and School literacies at The *Escuelita*: A Recipe for Engaged Asset-Based Learning." 2014. Unpublished Microsoft Word File.

Moll, Luis C. "Literacy research in community and classrooms: A sociocultural approach." *Theoretical Models and Processes of Reading*. 4th edition. Robert B. Ruddell and Norma Unrau Eds. Robert B. Ruddell and Harry Singer Newark: International Reading Association, 1994. Print.

Moll, Luis C., Cathy Amanti, Deborah Neff and Norma Gonzalez. "Funds of Knowledge for Teaching: Using a Qualitative Approach to Connect Homes and Classrooms." *Theory into Practice. Qualitative Issues in Educational Research* 31.2 (1992) : 132-141. Print.

Moll, Luis C. and James B. Greenberg. "Creating zones of possibilities: Combining Social contexts for instruction." V*ygotsky and Education: Instructional Implication and Applications of Sociohistorical Psychology*. Ed. Luis C. Moll London: Cambridge UP, 1992. 319 - 348. Print.

Miller, John W. "Overall Rankings," Central Connecticut State University, 2013.Web. 30 May 2015.

Philips, Sharon K, Melani W. Duffrin and Eugene A. Geist. "Be a Food Scientist." *Science and Children* 41.4 (2004) : 224-29. Web. 31 May 2015.

Scenters-Zapico, John. Generaciones' Narratives. Logan: Utah State UP, 2010. Electronic.

Schilb, John. "Special Focus: Food." *College English* 70.4 (2008) : 345- 436.

Seiler, Gale. "Reversing the "standard" direction: Science emerging from the lives of African American students." *Journal of Research in Science Teaching*, 38.9 (2001) : 1000–1014.

Sepulveda, Enrique. "Overcoming Deficit Thinking." *CT News Junkie*, 17 Sep 2012. Web. 30 May 2015.

Simmons, W.M. *Participation and power: Civic discourse in environmental policy decisions*. New York: SUNY, 2007. Print.

U.S. Census Bureau. "State and County QuickFacts: El Paso County, Texas." The United States Census Bureau, 22 Apr. 2015. Web. 28 May 2015.

Vélez-Ibáñez, Carlos G. and James B. Greenberg. "Formation and Transformation of Funds of Knowledge among U.S. Mexican Households." *Anthropology and Education Quarterly* 23.4 (1992) : 313-335. Print.

Yosso, Tara J. "Whose culture has capital? A critical race theory discussion of community cultural wealth." *Race Ethnicity and Education* 8.1 (2005) : 69-91. Web. 18 May 2015.

Author Bios

Dr. Lucía Durá is Assistant Professor of Rhetoric and Composition in the Department of English at The University of Texas at El Paso (UTEP). Her research focuses on innovative approaches to organizational and social change, intercultural communication, risk communication, and the discourses of health and medicine. Her recent work on positive deviance and intercultural communication has yielded numerous peer-reviewed presentations and publications. She is currently working on several positive deviance projects that combine education and race critical theory.

Consuelo Carr Salas is a fourth year doctoral candidate at the University of Texas at El Paso. She is the inaugural recipient of the Centennial Outstanding Doctoral Student Strauss Research Fellowship from the Department of English. Her research interests include visual rhetoric and the intersection of food studies and rhetoric.

Dr. Medina-Jerez is an Associate Professor of Science Education in the Department of Teacher Education at the University of Texas-El Paso (UTEP); he teaches undergraduate science methods courses, as well as graduate level courses on science teaching in bilingual classrooms. Before moving to UTEP, he was an Assistant Professor of Science Education at the University of Wyoming for five years, and before that he completed his post-doctoral appointment at Arizona State University (ASU) in both the College of Education and the Schools of Life Sciences. While at ASU, Dr. Medina-Jerez collaborated in research projects related to the use of technology in elementary school classrooms with English Language Learners (ELLs) (College of Education), and in aggression behavior studies of house finches (School of Life Sciences). Dr. Medina-Jerez earned his Ph.D. (2005) and M.S. (2002) in Science Education from the University of Iowa.

Ms. Hill has been with the Housing Authority of the City of El Paso for the past six years working as a Resident Relations Specialist. Prior to working with HACEP she worked for the Workforce Centers for 18 years. Ms. Hill has spent almost 25 years working with low and very low income persons assisting and encouraging them to leave public assistance and become self-sufficient. She believes children are the future of this nation, and that our current education system needs to change to allow them to lead the world.

Mindful Persistence: Literacies for Taking up and Sustaining Fermented-Food Projects[1]

Christina Santana, Stacey Kuznetsov, Sheri Schmeckpeper, Linda J. Curry, Elenore Long, Lauren Davis, Heidi Koerner, and Kimberly Butterfield McQuarrie

Almost by definition, resisting the insidious convenience of the mainstream food supply requires persistence. This is especially true for food projects requiring fermentation—projects that unfold over days or weeks and require day-to-day science in kitchens where variables can be hard to control and where some degree of periodic failure is almost inevitable. In this article, a team of writers—scholars and community members—dramatizes a joint inquiry from which emerged a composite portrait of what we have come to call *mindful persistence*—an existential yet collaborative engine that drives our food literacies. Dialogic text features highlight the situated insights of individual writers, indicating that while this team shares an interest in fermentation, this interest does not require or assume identical understandings of the science of fermentation or similar positions in the probiotic debate surrounding contemporary fermentation practices. Instead, what is shared is a mindful persistence that scaffolds reflective action in this dynamic problem space.

Introduction

Sheri: Six years ago a neighbor's boy was born allergic to food. He literally could not eat conventional food. He subsisted on nutrients fed through a feeding tube, and any attempt at feeding him solids or adding food to his tube would cause him great pain. At the age of four, the many doctors who had worked with his family said he would be gone within a year. Through research and reaching out, the parents learned about the GAPS (Gut and Psychology Syndrome) elimination diet and the benefits of an organic, non-processed diet. Within three months, he was off his feeding tube and eating seven solid foods. He is now a healthy boy who drinks cultured raw milk and eats organic meat and vegetables. He only exhibits symptoms when he eats foods produced in the traditional food chain.

Stories like Sheri's demonstrate the ineffectiveness of the current food system and how food-related literacy interventions can literally keep us alive. Not everyone shares a commitment to food literacy, but for my co-authors and me (Christina), our various food projects (i.e. fermenting,² pickling, urban farming, composting, bread making) have served as the impetus for several gatherings where we've shared what we know. We gathered together recently to share strategies for several food projects that involve fermentation: sauerkraut and kimchi, German and Korean techniques for fermenting cabbage with companion vegetables (see figure 1); kombucha, a fermented tea (see figure 2); and dairy kefir, milk fermented with a special culture (see figure 3). Experiences sharing fermentation projects have also prompted us to write together in a group that includes both academics at Arizona State University interested in fermented-food practices and community members (holding a range of academic degrees) engaged in a host of food projects, which in some cases form the foundation of our livelihoods.³

Persistence moves food-related knowledge into action, but persistence isn't often reflected upon in relation to food literacy. Consider, for instance, food-themed service-learning courses that embed students in "community-centered food service initiatives" for the purpose of engendering "powerful learning experience[s ...] that [are] emotionally and intellectually complex" (House 4). In a recent article for the *Community Literacy Journal*, Veronica House describes a course where students read food-themed texts (i.e. Holly Bauer's *Food Matters* or Brooke Rollins and Lee Bauknight's *Food*) to learn about issues related to the food movement (i.e. "relocalizing the food system" against the current delocalized food system). The course asks students "to think critically and to deeply explore, challenge and subvert the systemic, root causes of the manifested problems they see" (7). Such a course prepares students to answer the question, "Now what?" or "What will I do because of it?" (8). However, readers may wonder how, after the course, these students might persist in what they've learned about food as they live out their adult lives. Our paper asks what persistent food literacies may entail.⁴

Disciplinary commitments have propelled scholars to theorize persistence in the face of community-literacy projects that falter, for this is the nature of work with dynamic communities (Clifton 251). As scholars engaged with communities, we are primed to situate—"adapt" and "shape"—our best practices (Restaino 261). Fragile, provisional and responsive, community literacy requires persistence; such engagement mirrors the stamina, grit, and tenacity necessary to practice the food literacies of fermented-food projects. What's often missing from food-related peer-reviewed articles is attention to the work of everyday individuals who participate in local publics and circulate new knowledge within their spheres of influence (Higgins, Long and Flower 32). In response, we articulate mindful approaches that allow us to persist in taking up and sustaining food projects in the face of a broken food system.⁵

Methods of Joint Inquiry and Co-Authorship

In this article, we present findings from a two-part community conversation on food projects involving fermentation. Phase one began as a quotidian food science study that asked participants to allow Stacey and Christina to interview them in their own homes to understand their individual food-related practices, and culminated in a larger food workshop hosted by Stacey, Christina and Elenore. During the workshop, ten practitioners demonstrated techniques and shared expertise while making three fermented foods: sauerkraut, dairy kefir and kombucha. (See figures 1-3.) Sufficient supplies and elbowroom allowed all of us—even those in the group least familiar with food projects that involve fermentation (Christina and Elenore)—to participate in this first phase.

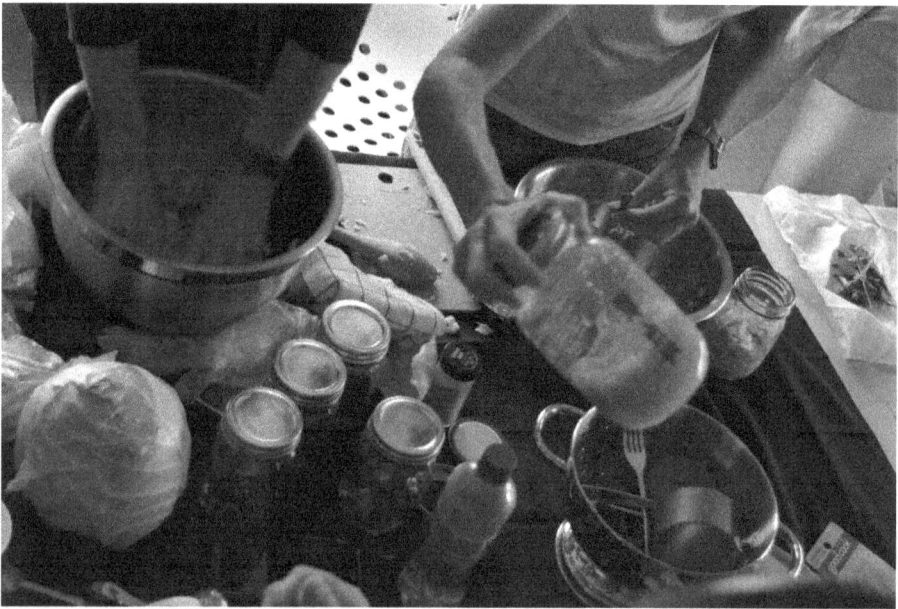

Figure 1: Participants share practices for making sauerkraut and kimchi—German and Korean techniques for fermenting cabbage with companion vegetables.

Figure 2: Bottles of a fermented tea called kombucha invite sampling during the first phase of a community conversation on fermented foods.

Figure 3: Participants add fresh fruit to dairy kefir—milk fermented with a special culture.

At the end of the food workshop, participants were invited to return the following week to meet as potential co-authors for The *Community Literacy Journal*'s special issue on food literacy.[6] For this second phase, four of the community members who had participated in the food workshop gathered for the express purpose of co-authoring this essay. To consider our purposes as co-authors, we—Stacey, Christina, Elenore—devised flexible, informal questions to prime the pump for our conversation:

• Why do you invest your time in food projects? What motivates you?

- What is the biggest challenge you face as someone experimenting with food? How do you persist beyond challenges?

- In interviews, nearly everyone mentioned reading other people's experiments with food projects--on blogs, discussion boards, and scholarly articles. When do you most often turn to these, and what do you gain from reading about other ideas and experiences with food projects?

To begin writing together, we each chose one of the above questions and drafted written responses for ten minutes. Then, adapting Kathy Charmaz's approach to grounded theorizing to our collaborative inquiry, Christina led the group discussion. Taking each of the above questions in turn, those responding to a given question took the first crack at articulating key points to map on the whiteboard. (See figure 4.) Before moving to the next question, the rest of us also contributed insights of our own—each of which was recorded in a different color on the whiteboard. (See appendix for Christina's second phase plan.) Afterwards, we consolidated insights around the themes we identified from the conversation (See figure 5).

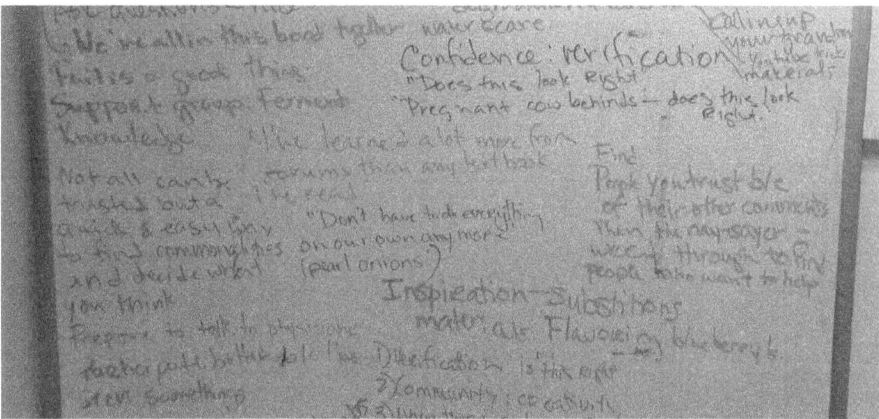

Figure 4: At the second phase of the community conversation, participants fill six whiteboards with responses to a set of key questions concerning their food practices.

Figure 5: Colored sticky notes identify themes emerging from the conversation.

What emerged was a portrait of *mindful persistence*, a concept that has become the focus of this paper and, thus, dramatized at length below. To be clear: some came to the group talking of mindfulness, and that term gained further resonance across the group as we talked. Also, one of the discussion questions focused explicitly on persistence, particularly persisting in one's food projects in the face of challenges. But the larger concept of *mindful persistence* emerged over the course of our sustained conversation. The dark sticky notes on the poster board in figure 5 highlight this concept emerging from the range of responses to the conversation's three key questions.[7]

Food Literacy as *Mindful* Raising, Growing, Preparing, and Eating

Many of us did not grow up with food literacies. We instead developed them as adults, as Lauren demonstrates below:

> Lauren: When it comes to food, like most others, I have inherited eating habits from my family. As a child, I believed that if doctors and dentists and my mother were giving me candy and treats when I was uncomfortable or in pain, they [these snacks] must have been safe and good for me. These inadvertent acts conditioned me as a child to seek such soothing with food for any unacceptable situation, and thus set the stage for what became a love-hate relationship with food. As an adult, I struggled to change food habits that I thought were the only ones available to me - after I began to experience my body and health breakdown. When I found myself overcome with food allergies, I realized that the food corporations I trusted would neither help me nor educate me. That was when I knew it was time to change my deeply ingrained conditioning—to know my food and own my choices.

Lauren's story demonstrates how mind*less* relationships to food can become ingrained unless they are consciously shifted by mind*ful* decisions made in adulthood. In the vice of personal responsibility, Lauren was faced with a harsh reality which lead her to investigate the deep-running and socially embedded roots of her thinking about food, especially the normative emotional connections she had accepted, to form a new foundation in which to cultivate a mindful approach to food that would inform the rest of her life.

In Western cultures, mindfulness is often thought of as a type of Buddhist meditation, which privileges "diligen[t] aware[ness …] to (1) the activity of the body, (2) sensations or feelings, (3) the activities of the mind, (4) ideas, thoughts, conceptions and things" (Rahula 48).[8] As secular practitioners, we are drawn to the concept of mindfulness as a mode of intervention that implements "a very particular mental state which is both wholesome and capable of clear and penetrating insight into the nature of reality" (Cullen 1). For us, mind*ful*ness resists dominant society's *mindless* approach to food—the expectation for perfect, sanitized foods, created to be the best looking with the fewest and cheapest inputs. Seen in this way, mindfulness springs from the work of being hands-on and present with our food and the relationships we recreate every time we sit down for a meal.

Also, we emphasize mindful persistence as a distinct and experimental way of knowing and doing food projects. An experimental way of knowing conjures a host of literacy scholars committed to wise action, scholars ranging from John Dewey to Paulo Freire to Linda Flower to Paul Lynch.[9] By practicing the food literacies we describe here, we persist in our practice of mindfulness in three ways: changing habits, sharing and collaborating, and managing risk in order to cultivate conditions for safety regarding our own food. These modes of engagement allow us to persist in our engagement with food. Below, food experts in our group bear witness to the unique dimensions of persistence enacted as mindful fermented-food literacies.

Changing Habits

As Lauren's above experience illustrates, when food becomes a motivating factor for change, it is no longer simply something that soothes the stomach and tickles the taste buds; rather, it becomes a resource for the functioning of a full life and for personal well-being. This means that our attitudes necessarily shift, sometimes dramatically, as we take up the experimental processes inherent in relocating food expertise from the seat of societal authorities to our individual kitchens. Changing habits cannot be expected to be comfortable. In the excerpt below, Kimberly explains how the consequences of her family's food choices outweighed the prior emphasis they'd placed on the taste or appearance of food. This shift in orientation gave Kimberly and her family the impetus they needed to persist in reorienting their food habits:

> Kimberly: Fermenting first began to change how we [Kim and her family] ate food. Processed foods began to dwindle from our diet. Eventually my whole family began to crave whole foods. As we added more fermented foods, our views rapidly changed. Now we see food in a new way. I no longer focus on how food tastes, smells or looks. I spend time researching what a food does. I enjoy knowing how foods react to one another. Often meals are prepared for how they will make me feel internally instead of mentally.

Kimberly's experience shows that by deliberately introducing a variety of fermented foods over time, her and her family's food habits have changed. Her current perceptions (i.e. her reactions to the tastes and sights of particular foods) and conceptions (i.e. what food should be doing for her) have become highly developed as a result of her commitment to food-related substance over form. This commitment reflects core aspects of Buddhist mindfulness: attention to body (habit), attention to sensation, attention to perception, attention to conception (Rahula 48). Because she is most attentive to what food is good for, at a conceptual level she is less perturbed by the unfamiliar sensations of taste, smell, and sight that her food projects introduce her to such as the Symbiotic Colony Of Bacteria and Yeast (or SCOBY) used for making the fermented tea called kombucha – and she is able to take full ownership of her food choices. (Images of SCOBY are below, figues 6 and 7.)

Figure 6 (left): Symbiotic Colony Of Bacteria and Yeast (or SCOBY) used in making the fermented tea called kombucha. Figure 7 (right): A piece of SCOBY culture is added to tea.

Kimberly's experience also indirectly points us to a second component of changing habits: the importance of rethinking the role of expertise in the context of our own lives. As Sheri explains below, recognizing contradictory or muddled arguments that circulate in society's authority systems can spur us to change food habits and to develop a greater sense of self-reliance when it comes to the food we eat:

> Sheri: Over the decades I've listened to the experts as they flip-flopped about what is good and what is bad for us, always stating their theories with great authority and presenting them as facts only to contradict themselves later. All this caused me to delve deeply into what and whom I really believe. How can I know what is right or wrong? I've learned about bacteria, yeasts, fungus, and molds. I've learned that only 1% of all bacteria are harmful ("Bacterial Infections"), yet listening to the words of the health experts and media, a germ is a germ, and it must be destroyed. This fear-based thinking has reinforced my resolve to question everything and to make choices intentionally, according to my unique needs and those of my family. My understanding of traditional food evolved into a belief system, a set of values, and as such, lifestyle changes are relatively easy. We now raise and produce 80% of our own food, including meat, dairy, and produce, and help others do the same comfortably, emphasizing freedom to explore within the boundaries of caution.

Sheri's experience shows that she was able to advance new food habits only after interrogating the logic of expertise, which she realized too heavily influenced the logic of her own thinking. For her, the fallibility of experts underscored that outside experts weren't the best or only decision-makers to rely on. By stripping away untrustworthy ideas, she was able to rely on her own logic and intuition. Now, Sheri rests assured in the revisable expertise she has developed by doing her own reading—expertise she has cultivated for herself, her family, and her students.

The family-oriented nature of Kimberly and Sheri's experiences shows how creating new food environments in the home can support changing food habits. Heidi's experience below goes further to show how new practices cultivated in our homes can support learning:

> Heidi: My biggest challenge is that I fail sometimes. I think that as I'm getting older, I have had a few birthdays, I'm ok with failing. My first sauerkraut failed miserably. But, you know? I just put it in the compost pile. Now, I set my house up so that there really isn't waste. When things go bad, I either feed them to the worms, or compost them. And my chickens will eat all kinds of mistakes—then give me poop that goes back into the ground. So I feel that if I fail, it's ok. It's ok.

Heidi's experience shows that as we start to do things differently, those activities might not go as well as planned. To allow for more intentional experimentation, Heidi reconfigured her home to productively reuse what otherwise would have been wasted. Her changed attitude toward waste is more attuned to ways that her multiple food projects can reinforce "an *ecology*, or things and forces joined together in dynamic coexistence, sustainable over time" (Rickert 248). By paying attention to and discovering the links of the food chain as they exist in her own home, Heidi manages the challenge of failure efficiently.

Habits that are deeply ingrained in the body and mind are difficult to change, but that change becomes possible, even inevitable, when the mindset about food (its creation, its processing and preparation, and its effect) becomes personalized. Often, food habits don't change on the basis of averages, norms, dictates or expert opinions. Rather, as food becomes a personalized component of an individual's life, her choices result in consequences she experiences first hand. Now habits become more than involuntary responses; they become intentional behaviors, the available means for mindful persistence.

Sharing and Collaboratively Constructing Mindful Practices

At least in Western paradigms, mindfulness can evoke hyper-individualism; in contrast, we use *mindful persistence* to invoke a relation *with* others. Regarding participants' fermented-food projects, the mind, as a metaphor of the individual, gets rewritten as a source of collective wisdom.

> Linda: My teaching program will in fact focus on convenience, but it still means spending more time in the kitchen. Preparing whole foods, however you chop it up, is still going to take longer than popping open a bag of potato chips. This is where mindfulness comes in. When we truly clear our minds

and are present with what our body needs, preparing a salad becomes a moving meditation. Teaching mindfulness is not always easy however. The way I move in the demonstrations and how I sit to sample each food item with the class is key. My voice slows. I put my fork down after I take a bite, and I set the stage for the energy at the table. Students quickly feel the pace and partake in the nourishment. My students often feel refreshed and better about food in general. Small experiences like this give them tools to take home and are key to slowly integrating new healthier habits.

Linda shows how she conducts herself during her "From Processed Foods to Whole Foods" classes in order to show that whole foods affect more than the palate. By modeling a way of being with food that is punctuated, she enacts what she knows, instantiating abstract concepts about health with a mindful approach to healthier alternatives. Because she explicitly calls this work "teaching mindfulness," she makes it a point to thoughtfully demonstrate to her students exactly how to "pay attention in a particular way: on purpose, in the present moment, and nonjudgmentally" (Kabat-Zinn 4, qtd. in Cullen 2).

In contrast, Lauren experiences mindful sharing and collaboration online and informally in groups of peers. Sharing affinities for particular food projects, participants encourage one another to explore food and to share successes and failures non-judgmentally as a means of developing the group's social cohesion. Below, Lauren explains how her participation with these forums encourages her to persist in her food projects:

> Lauren: I belong to fermentation groups, vegetarian groups, trade/swap groups, and chicken-keeping groups on Facebook. There, I've met others who support my successes and failures. They are "support groups" that give advice freely and share from their experiences. They allow you to pick and choose from suggestions comprising a wealth of knowledge. Learning from other's failures makes you realize you are not alone, and if there is a mistake to be made, someone else has already made it and is very willing to share the outcome with you. Reading a book is one thing, but being able to ask questions in real time from someone more experienced is like being able to ask your great-grandmother that same question.

Above, Lauren describes sharing her mistakes in supportive groups, thus highlighting two features of mindful persistence. First, group participation lets her transform private information about an error she's made into something potentially valuable to others—something that others, as well as she, herself, can learn to avoid more efficiently by collaboratively naming and theorizing what went awry. Second, Lauren characterizes food-orientated online affinity groups as highly accessible stores of collective wisdom. As Lauren puts it, the invocation of an idealized great-grandmother organizes and informs persistence against mind-less food practices.

Lauren's experience begins to show us how mindful persistence seeks others as resources for wise practice. Below, Linda narrates cultivating this orientation upon moving to Phoenix—a harsh environment that required her not only to rethink her approach to gardening but to retool her repertoire as a gardener:

> Linda: Sharing garden harvests with neighbors is a great way to not only trade produce, but to learn from each other as well. Neighbors that have been in your area a while tend to know what the critters may like or leave alone. Moving into a desert area, I had to re-learn gardening by learning from the critters (rabbit, quail, javelina) as well as my neighbors who saved me a lot of heartache, trial and error.

The wisdom of others, including both animals and people, enlivened Linda's adjustment to the desert. Expertise in this context is not dogmatic but rather nuanced, experimental, and situated in terms of what food projects work for individuals within the affordances and constraints of their own lives. This nuanced and shared approach to information permits people to persist in pursuing a mindful approach to food.

Managing Risk, Cultivating Conditions for Safety

Introducing microbes into the human body—as fermented foods do—requires an experimental way of knowing. On the one hand, this work behooves us to understand as best we can the conditions in which we are working, in this case, the status of our physical bodies. Along this same vein, this work also behooves us to understand our interventions, in this case, fermented food projects, well enough to know the changes they introduce. On the other hand fermented-food literacies embrace sometimes highly complex experimentation in our own kitchens, so outcomes can thwart our best predictions. Figuratively speaking, managing risk and cultivating conditions for safety do not mean that if you are allergic to bees you cannot be a beekeeper, but they do mean that you must know how to manage the risk of and response to being stung.

Part of what makes managing risk so difficult and so important is that different people experience the risks associated with fermentation differently. Below, Linda and Sheri explain:

> Linda: One challenge for me is making sure that we're not making people sick. If I share this with my family, say, someone who WILL take antibiotics every time they get sick, they may not have the gut to handle a little bit of mold where I might be able to handle it. People do have concerns for some good reasons because in our society today, they're all on antibiotics if they're eating meat from a factory farm, so they might not be able to handle raw dairy or some bacteria.

Sheri: The liquid in sauerkraut is a lactobacillus bacteria that preserves the cabbage. Anything above the liquid level may become moldy (start to decay) and can be removed. However, when it comes to the mold on sauerkraut, more than likely it will taste and smell so bad that a person will not consume it.

Schemas can cultivate unfounded fear about molds, and they inhibit mindful persistence. In fact, some of us participating in this community conversation on food fermentation grew up with mothers practicing (largely out of the necessity not to waste food from the weekly trip to the grocery store) a healthy respect for mold in their fridges and breadboxes. But the lure of sanitized, sterile pre-packaged food led us to build our own schemas about mold that inhibited an interest in or a willingness to experiment with fermentation until learning about the need to engage the science of contemporary food practices for ourselves.

Below, Linda and Sheri enter into a dialogue about experimentation. The juxtaposition of their two approaches to experimentation is an argument for mindful persistence, illustrating that food literacies need not insist on conforming to a single ideology or set of practices. Rather, mindful persistence in the domain of fermented-foods is attentive to risk, including the risk of exposing ourselves, friends, and clients to bacteria and other organisms that their intestinal systems may have difficulty adjusting to, considering all bodies are different. First, Linda describes how she cultivates conditions for safety without discouraging experimentation or fearing the inevitable failed experiment:

Linda: Preparation techniques are critical with fermenting foods as you need the right environment, equipment and quality ingredients to make it work. For example, when making cultured vegetables or fermented pickles that use a closed system (i.e. mason jar), it is essential that no air will get in the jar. Also, carbon dioxide needs to escape. There are special jars for this that do not let oxygen in—that could create mold. In addition, if you are not using organic non-GMO [genetically modified organism] ingredients, you may be doing more harm to your health than good. Temperature and light also play a part in fermentation. As the seasons change, you may need to make adjustments to the duration of your project or place the mason jars in warmer/cooler locations. In addition, covering mason jars with a towel to avoid sunlight is pertinent. Because fermentation deals with bacteria and yeast, things can go south if you're not on top of the food experiments happening in your kitchen. Mold and bad yeasts can easily develop in your food without your knowing it. Simply scraping mold from food is a dangerous practice that some currently practice. Understanding the science behind fermentation and finding the best methods are important measures to ensuring we are adding to our health, not hindering it. Besides understanding the science, sniffing food experiments has become a ritual in my household for additional confidence. I have first-hand knowledge of how to explode a jar of sauerkraut and smell up the kitchen. Constant research and experimentation is part of the journey to creating amazing nutritionally rich foods.

Next, Sheri dramatizes a mindful approach that re-sees microorganisms as contributors to health:

> Sheri: I think we can all relate strongly to Linda's explosive experience! Explosions, in my case, a spray of carrot juice foam fountaining all over the kitchen, are both memorable moments and learning opportunities. The truly dangerous failures are rare events. More often, we find ourselves with unexpected outcomes. I recently tried preserving radishes in kombucha. Rather than preserving them, it consumed them, and I ended up with a liquid that was filled with radish particles and skins. I've made batches of cheese that tasted like bread because bread yeast was still in the air when I pressed the cheese. With those outcomes, we find alternative uses—dog and chicken food, compost, etc. Safety can mean anything from using glass containers to avoid leaching of BPAs [synthetic compounds found in plastics] or contaminants that might have been absorbed into plastics, while taking precautions to avoid breaking fragile glass containers, to being cautious about consuming any questionable foods. Botulism and other foodborne illnesses are not to be taken lightly. Cultures that are strange in behavior or appearance should be questioned. A body that has been stripped of natural microbes must introduce new ones with care.
>
> As Linda noted, smelling becomes part of the process. In fact, all senses become attuned to what characteristics food should present. Touching, tasting, smelling, observing, and even listening for the right crunch or the right effervescence becomes second nature. A healthy environment has to ensure that the microbes are happy and there is no cross-pollination between cultures or between an intended culture and an undesired infiltrator. We cannot eliminate yeasts, fungi, or bacteria because food experiments depend on these microorganisms for success.

Linda's and Sheri's approaches to safe experimental practices aren't about eradicating microorganisms from food but rather about wisely approaching their roles in food preservation and digestion. Sheri explains an appeal she employs to reorient others toward risks that fermented-foods introduce:

> Sheri: I emphasize in my classes that we must remember that we would be without life if it were not for these little organisms breaking down the larger components of dead matter into smaller ones, ultimately creating building blocks for new life. In my world, I intentionally grow bacteria and yeast

cultures. I consume them to strengthen my body. In the process of working my cows' manure and other decaying matter that brings life naturally to my garden, I expose myself to unknown numbers of microorganisms. I compost vegetation, intentionally growing bacteria, enzymes, and little creatures—all species working hand-in-hand as they have done for millennia. I do this because I believe in it.

As members of this informal food collective, we have talked a lot about the ways that convenience has taken over in our country; as a consequence, basic knowledge about food, digestion, and immunity is being lost. Part of what is lost is an experimental approach to food that acknowledges legitimate concerns—i.e., concerns that some bacteria can be harmful—while cultivating a healthy respect for experimentation in the kitchen that is attentive to practices that keep food safe. Such an orientation is mindful about not only our own health, here and now, but also the well-being of our future generations' health and the health of our planet.

Conclusion

We may not be able to convince every person that store-bought chicken eggs also come out of the back of a chicken, or that kombucha SCOBYs are worth celebrating, but mindful persistence can rhetorically orient us toward becoming living examples of health. In the context of food literacy, mindful persistence is an individual journey travelled within a community. This journey is an intentional quest to build ongoing health and to address individual and familial health problems by practicing culinary techniques not necessarily acknowledged by conventional expertise. While fermented-food projects may appear to some as a potentially dangerous game, when done well, they can transform what we consume into medicinal gifts that are healthy and nutritive. At its best, mindful persistence—as a way in the world practiced with others—provides the guidance, structure, and cautions needed to experiment safely, whether or not the experiment results in failure or success. This one-to-one and one-to-many communication fosters the mindful persistence that fermented-food literacies demand.

Endnotes

1. We'd like to thank the following contributors for their participation in the first phase of the community conversation: Kris Bullock, Katie DiBenedetto, Riley McPherson, Bob Schmeckpeper, and Carrie Weldy.

2. Fermented foods are sometimes referred to as cultured foods.

3. As everyday food scientists, we turn our kitchens into grassroots laboratories in an effort to approach food as a deliberate practice that includes observation, experimentation, explication, and documentation.

4. In collaborating as a group of community and university scholars as we do here, we seek to contribute to a growing body of scholarship that emerges from the community and is considered valuable for the work it does, not for the institutional engine that has produced it. For example, in *Reclaiming our Food: How the Grassroots Food Movement is Changing the Way We Eat*, Tanya Denckla Cobb describes many things "[w]e are moving away from" and "toward" as a way of "rebuilding local food systems" (8). She argues that food and community are in fact intertwined, that "a community can grow a more sustainable and resilient economy by growing its local food system, and a healthy local food system will nurture and grow community spirit" (9). Though Cobb's text is not peer-reviewed, her work has been cited 20 times according to Google Scholar by scholars writing about sustainable, community-based urban practices.

5. Here, we foreground mindful persistence in response to *Community Literacy Journal*'s call for papers on community food literacies. This decision means that other relevant domains of knowledge about fermentation—including the science and public controversy concerning probiotics—remain in the background of this article.

6. This opportunity came as a surprise to participants who had only expected to share their food related knowledge with like-minded others willing and able to attend the food workshop (hosted at 1:00 p.m. on a Thursday).

7. With an outline generated at the end of the workshop in hand, Christina moved the working draft to Google Drive where participants had access as co-authors. The analysis constructed a dynamic and dialogical "we" from claims about mindful persistence that participants articulated together over the course of the co-authoring workshop, which was audio recorded, and the Google Drive drafting space. The majority of insights about mindful persistence conveyed in the commentary were jointly constructed over the course of our community conversation and work online regarding this paper; thus, these insights belong to the group more than to any individual. In contrast, specific names are ascribed to particular individuals' experiences and situated knowledge, and, in the case of Christina, to her efforts to frame, launch, and sustain this writing project.

8. Special thanks to Robert LaBarge for providing us with access to his collection of Buddhist works.

9. Metaphorically speaking this "experimental way of knowing" can be said to support a kind of intellectual fermentation. However, our focus here is on the more literal practice of sustained inquiry with fermented foods.

Works Cited

Bauer, Holly, ed. *Food Matters: A Bedford Spotlight Reader*. Boston: Bedford/St. Martin's, 2014. Print.

Bowen, Lauren Marshall, et al. "Community Engagement in a Graduate-Level Community Literacy Course." *Community Literacy Journal* 9.1 (2014): 18-38. Web.

Charmaz, Kathy. *Constructing Grounded Theory*. 2nd ed. New York: Sage, 2014. Print.

Clifton, Jennifer. "Outreach as a Stochastic Art: Lessons Learned with the Sudanese Diaspora in Phoenix." Ed. Jessica Restaino and Laurie JC Cella. *Unsustainable: Re-imagining Community Literacy, Public Writing, Service-Learning, and the University*. Lanham: Lexington Books, 2013. 227-52. Print.

Cobb, Tanya Denckla. *Reclaiming Our Food: How the Grassroots Food Movement is Changing the Way We Eat*. North Adams: Storey Publishing, 2011. Print.

Cullen, Margaret. "Mindfulness-based Interventions: An Emerging Phenomenon." *Mindfulness* 2.3 (2011): 186-93. Web.

Dewey, John. *The Quest for Certainty*. Vol. 4 of *John Dewey: The Later Works, 1925–1953*. Ed. Jo Ann Boydston. Carbondale: Southern Illinois UP, 1988. Print.

Flower, Linda. *Community Literacy and the Rhetoric of Public Engagement*. Carbondale: Southern Illinois UP, 2008. Print.

Freire, Paulo. *Pedagogy of the Oppressed*. New York: Bloomsbury Publishing, 2000. Print.

Higgins, Lorraine, Elenore Long and Linda Flower. "Community Literacy: A Rhetorical Model for Personal and Public Inquiry." *Community Literacy Journal* 1.1 (2006): 9-42. Print.

House, Veronica. "Re-Framing the Argument: Critical Service-Learning and Community-Centered Food Literacy." *Community Literacy Journal* 8.2 (2014): 1-16. Web.

Lynch, Paul. *After Pedagogy: The Experience of Teaching*. New York: NCTE, 2013. Print.

Rahula, Walpola. *What the Buddha Taught: Revised and Expanded Edition with Texts from Suttas and Dhammapada*. New York, NY: Grove, 1974. Print.

Restaino, Jessica, "Conclusion: Rejecting Binaries and Rethinking Relationships." *Unsustainable: Re-imagining Community Literacy, Public Writing, Service-Learning and the University*. Ed. Jessica Restaino and Laurie JC Cella. Lanham: Lexington Books, 2013. 253-62. Print.

Rickert, Thomas. *Ambient Rhetoric: The Attunements of Rhetorical Being*. Pittsburgh: U of Pittsburgh P, 2013. Print.

Rollins, Brooke and Lee Bauknight, eds. *Food*. Southlake: Fountain Head P, 2010. Print.

U.S. National Library of Medicine. "Bacterial Infections." U.S. Department of Health and Human Services, 19 May 2015. Web. 1 June 2015.

Appendix: Food Co-authoring Community Conversation (Phase 2)

Christina: Welcome and introductions

- Ask *everyone* to briefly explain their own food projects, and what made them interested in attending the food writing workshop.
- Introduce the three questions, and explain that we're going to talk about all of them together: "For starters, please pick one question and take 5 to 10 minutes to prepare your thoughts with some notes."
    - Q1: Why do you invest your time in food projects? What motivates you?
    - Q2: What is the biggest challenge you face as someone experimenting with food? How do you persist beyond the challenge?
    - Q3: In interviews, everyone or nearly everyone mentioned reading other people's experiences with food projects—on blogs, discussion boards, scholarly articles. When do you most often turn to these, what do you gain from reading about other ideas and experiences with food projects?

Christina: Initiate and facilitate sharing

- Ask someone to start the conversation: "Did anyone take up the first question?"

Elenore and Stacey: Write ideas on whiteboards in three "question columns"

- Listen and ask before writing: "Where would you like this on the board *top right*? *bottom left*?"
    - The goal here is to create initial spatial relationships even though the first few people may resist this prompt. We should assist in grouping like ideas with placement, circles, lists ...
- Ask *everyone* - in turn - to contribute answers to the first question.
- Wait in silence before moving on to the second question and ask: "Is there anything else we want to add up here?"
- Ask someone to start the conversation about the second question then the third.

Christina: Review CLJ Call for Papers (CFP)

- Call attention to specific lines of text to explain that our ideas (on the whiteboards) will give us what we need for the journal article, i.e.,: "What role does food literacy play in our communities?"
    - or—How or why does what you and others do (read, write, teach, learn or share) with food matter?: "What role does community literacy play in local and global food movements?"
    - or—How do local and global food movements impact what you do (read, write, teach, learn or share) with others?

Christina: Show example of collaborative article w/annotation (Bowen et al.)

- Explain that the article is written by a professor and her graduate students: "This is a class where students learn about what it takes (practically and conceptually) to work with people outside of the university" (19).
- Explain that the article is largely structured by themes they've identified in their context - a good model for us: "The hands-on experiences allowed them to 'critically reflect' on their experiences and identify themes with which to draft their own sections " (19).
    - The themes show *some* of what is scholarly-relevant to community literacy studies: Reciprocity, Problem-solving Pragmatics, Ethics, Sustainability

Christina: Move the conversation back to the white boards

- Ask someone to start identifying themes by way of the model text: "Let's try to identify or construct some themes *together* by looking back at our responses to the three questions we started with."
    - The goal here is to let people speak back to what one another ventures when they're naming things by writing ideas on whiteboards at the bottom of the three "question columns", assisting in identifying relationships among themes, and consolidating themes on the poster board to articulate possible emerging logics.
- Ask everyone to think about drafting: "Is there one of these themes that *anyone* would like to commit to drafting?"
- Ask section managers to invite participation (via email) and commit to deadlines.

Author Bios

Christina Santana is a PhD Candidate in the Writing, Rhetorics and Literacies program at Arizona State University. She is currently working on her dissertation, entitled *Deliberating the Future of Driving in an Intentionally-Mediated Space*, a project which offers the literate practice of "framing"—inspired by Kenneth Burke's frames of acceptance and rejection—for the purpose of fostering productive speculation. She is also interested in the behind-the-scenes work of community writing for scholarly purposes.

Stacey Kuznetsov is an assistant professor at the School of Arts, Media, and Engineering (AME) with a joint appointment at the School of Computing, Informatics, and Decision Systems Engineering (CIDSE) at Arizona State University. Her research explores the role of technology in collective efforts to construct knowledge and address issues. She is interested in low-cost tools and hands-on making for citizen science, community activism, and DIY biology.

Sheri Schmeckpeper lives on a 1.25 acre family farm, where she and her husband, Bob, produce nearly 80% of their food, including vegetables, fruit, meat, and dairy. Since completing her career in higher education, Sheri has been able to pursue her passion for teaching, writing, and coaching others about food production, processing, and preservation. Sheri acknowledges the wisdom inherent in nature, and thus emphasizes the use of natural methods and sciences in her classes and her life.

Linda J. Curry is a plant-based cooking instructor and health advisor. She teaches individual and group instruction in Mesa, Arizona. In addition, she manufactures a natural skin care line called *Simple Nature Skincare*.

Elenore Long is an associate professor of community literacy at Arizona State University. With Lorraine Higgins and Linda Flower, she co-authored the lead article for the inaugural issue of Community Literacy Journal. She is currently working on a book project entitled *Makahda: Are we still in this: A Responsive Rhetorical Art for Local Public Life*. She serves on the Board of Directors for the Nile Institute for Peace and Development, a transnational consortium responsive to historic trauma, a globalized economy, changing demographics, and shrinking public resources.

Lauren Davis belongs to fermentation groups, heritage turkey groups, vegetarian groups, trade/swap groups, and chicken-keeping groups on Facebook.

Heidi Koerner received a BS in Psychology from Arizona State University and a Doctorate in Naturopathic Medicine from Southwest College of Naturopathic Medicine. She is currently enrolled in a concurrent nursing program with Northern Arizona University and Gateway Community College.

Kimberly Butterfield McQuarrie is a mom, wife, sister, cancer survivor, and fermenter. As a mother of three boys, she especially tries to eat and live clean. Surviving cancer has inspired her to keep fighting and to teach those around her to live better with less.

Sponsors of Agricultural Literacies: Intersections of Institutional and Local Knowledge in a Farming Community

Marcy L. Galbreath

> Many of the agricultural literacies engendering twentieth-century farming practices and shaping contemporary concepts of food and nutrition in the United States arose through scientific research at land-grant colleges. This article examines how those literacies reached and interacted with local communities through institutional entities such as the extension service and its youth program, the 4-H.

It is easy to forget, while browsing the produce section of the local supermarket, how close to home food production once was. Vegetables and fruits now make their way to American tables from many points of the globe, providing convenience and a reduced dependence on seasonality. The literacies associated with this plenitude are complex, especially if we think of how deeply food is connected to ideologies of production and consumption. Food literacy touches on understandings of what food means to a particular culture, how it originates, how it fits into the supply chain, and how it is marketed, prepared, and consumed, among other things. One way to unpack at least some of this complexity is to consider the genesis of the modern agricultural system at the level of an agricultural community and to explore how institutional ideas of food production were shared with small-scale truck farmers.[1] Food literacy, from the perspective of the farmer, can be understood as agricultural literacy—an acquired knowledge that comes from experiential actions as well as written texts.[2] My research examines oral histories and archival materials to see how twentieth-century agricultural literacy, arising in the scientific research at the land-grant colleges, was transmitted to local farming communities. I argue that this literacy movement is a recursive, responsive process evident in the transitional space where the institutions of the extension service and its youth program, the 4-H, interfaced with local farming communities.

The community at the center of this research, Samsula, is a small rural community in Central Florida located in Volusia County. Samsula became a site of agricultural production in the early twentieth century during the Florida land boom. This was also a period of transformation for agriculture in the United States as federal and state governments became involved in creating a more profit-oriented agricultural sector. The legislative actions of the First Morrill Act, the Hatch Act, and the Smith-Lever Act, respectively, created the land-grant college system, regional experiment stations, and the extension service to research and implement new methods and technologies of farm production.³ Modernizing developments from these institutions included chemical technologies for controlling insects and disease, new understandings of soil composition and improvement, and emerging technologies for cultivating land. Modernization also meant running a farm on a budget, keeping records of profits and losses, and tracking weather, crop outcomes, and expenses—in short, treating farming like a regular business. For the primarily Slovenian immigrants who moved to Samsula in the early part of the century, agriculture was the economic mainstay of the community—it was necessary to approach it as a business for the community to survive. Some of the descendants of those early settlers continue the farming tradition today, and these are the subjects who agreed to participate in my study.⁴

Agricultural Literacies and Their Sponsors

While the early Samsula community was quite isolated geographically, local farmers still had connections to the modernizing influences of the era and thus to the organizations and institutions that carried nascent agricultural literacies. In her seminal 1998 article, Deborah Brandt argues that literacy can be viewed as a commodity, and that those who provide literate skills—the "sponsors"—stand to gain something in the exchange (166, 169). In the twentieth-century history of U.S. farming, government institutions such as the USDA and extension service were among the external entities who shaped agricultural practices and who can be considered sponsors of agricultural literacy.⁵ Literacy sponsors, as Brandt points out, also bring "ideological freight" as part of the process of literacy transfer: the resultant literacy practices reflect the perspectives, and thus may serve the interests, of the sponsors who transmit the ideas and skills associated with literate behavior (168). In the context of modernization, early justifications of institutional involvement in agricultural practices (including behaviors that can be seen as sponsorship) were promoted as avenues to economic stability.⁶ At the local level, this exchange is revealed as a more complex process, with various exigencies and individual agendas among the participating communities. The give and take of agricultural literacy transfer occurs within multiple rhetorical situations, and literacy sponsors from outside local communities must coexist with the more local sponsors such as family, neighbors, teachers, and customers.⁷

In the Samsula community, various sources of sponsorship have existed over time, each of whom might regard literate functionality somewhat differently. To the extension service agents, for example, the ability of those they sponsor to understand the promotional genres that explain the agency's ideas, methods, and materials might satisfy the criteria of agricultural literacy. At the same time, local farmers were exposed to more than one kind of agricultural literacy as they negotiated their relationships with the extension service agent, supply vendors, customers, and each other. The agricultural literacies of the working farmer came from learning based in observation and interactions with family, neighbors, outside sponsors, and direct experience with the soil, water, insects, and other location-specific factors impacting agriculture.

Farmers utilized these literacies to remain resilient and adapt to the fluid variables affecting their efforts, including market fluctuations and bad weather.

Extension service agents shared some common literacies with the farmers and vendors, and other kinds of agricultural literacies that enabled them to negotiate the texts and instructions coming from the land-grant college system and legislative bodies. The literacies of the extension agents arose from institutional expectations of specialist knowledge and included formal training and mentoring by other members of the extension service community. As conduits of science-based research, agents were expected to translate findings from the experiment station, such as the effects of a new pesticide, and to know enough about the chemistry and environmental factors to put it into language local farmers could use. Agent's literacies were reflective of the most up-to-date technologies available; in addition, they needed to be well versed in the specific local situations with which they were dealing.

The multiple systems of modern agriculture—land-grant colleges, extension service, experiment stations, agricultural supply companies, chemical companies, and local farming communities—each represent a different rhetorical situation; while separate, they connect with one another in areas of interactivity or contact zones.[8] The communications taking place in these contact zones are dynamic, changing and responding to economic situations, political influences, and environmental fluxes. The texts many of these systems use can help us map the interactions between communities and institutions; furthermore, the sites where writings from different rhetorical systems intersect and overlap can offer insights into the activities and motivations of literacy sponsors. In the Samsula farming community, the diffusion of agricultural literacies from the extension service and the understandings agents gained from practicing farmers met in a reciprocal contact zone—a generative intersection for agricultural adaptation.[9]

Local Agricultural Literacies

The interviews I conducted reveal that farmers primarily learn the basics of their craft and the accompanying agricultural literacy by immersion: they learn at the feet of others, as children, or they come into it as a community experience. Agricultural science as a formal educational venue is not the main source of understandings, since children growing up in farming families learn the ins and outs of raising produce by participating in farm work. Retired farmer Joe Bavec, a second-generation Samsula farmer, recalled an average after-school experience from his childhood:

> ... so you'd get home, you'd gulp down two glasses of milk, big plate full of cookies, but then you was expected to be out in the field, with a wheelbarrow, you pushed the wheelbarrow, you loaded the collard greens on it, or whatever, you pushed it up to the barn, put them in the cold water, keep them good and fresh, then worked them up and down, took them and stacked them on the cart, laid them twelve in a row, so we knew exactly how many dozen we had ... that was something I did every day.

Learning to farm came with the milk and cookies; it was just a part of life. The experience shapes the understanding of farming practices, and agricultural literacy in this description includes keeping count and keeping the greens "good and fresh" so they did not wilt.

Functional agricultural literacy also includes understanding and working with the technologies of modern farming. Some of the early settlers brought mechanical skillsets to the community from prior occupational experience, yet others gained knowledge from institutional sponsors through vocational agriculture school or 4-H programs. Samsula farmers did not call on a local mechanic shop for help when their machinery had problems but learned, primarily from other community members, how to maintain and repair their tractors, irrigation equipment, and other essential machinery. This knowledge was freely shared, as retired farmer Tony Vadnal recalled. He discussed starting out on his own, when "… there was always somebody that would help you out a little bit, we had a lot of exchange of equipment … other farmers would help out if you needed something, and especially if you were a young farmer that didn't have all that stuff." Vadnal's recollection helps us understand agricultural literacy in a community like Samsula as "collective knowledge" that is shared through both written and oral narratives, built upon and passed down from generation to generation, neighbor to neighbor.[10] While each farmer may have sustained an individual business, there was also a common interest in communal success. Learning acquired at an early age with the family is eventually extended, shared, and modeled by interactions with other community members through everyday discourses.

References to reading about how to farm are rare in my interviews, but descriptions of planting, cultivating, weeding, watering, picking, cleaning, packing, and selling abound. Anecdotes about practical farm experience, such as Bavec's and Vadnal's memories, convey tacit learning practices, as novice farmers learn by watching and doing. Agricultural literacies in these contexts mean reading the land, weather, plants, technologies, and people—understanding the environments, economies, and discourses within which agricultural works are conducted. An understanding of agricultural literacy thus shifts according to who is rendering it, and creates a tension between experiential understandings and what one farmer referred to as "by the book" knowledge.

Experiential stores of knowledge may count as a form of agricultural literacy not only for the farmer involved in them, but also for those external agents who benefit from the knowledge gained through such practice. As farmers performed the methods and technologies shared by the extension service, agents could see how these ideas worked. This recursive exchange illustrates the intersections or contact zones where local literacies overlapped with the literacies of the experiment stations. Techniques, new products, and innovative farm tools may be tested under controlled situations at the experiment stations, but it is not until they are tested in the real-world situation of a working farm that all participants know whether they will be effective. Farmers' fields served as open-air laboratories for these ideas; as Bavec observed, "it was feedback both ways … they have experimental farms … But they'll have a 10 by 10 plot, You know, you go look at a 10 acre or an acre [field], you get a lot more realistic view than that little 10 by 10 plot." The current extension service agent, Mary Sanderson, puts it even more succinctly, noting that the experiment stations actually rely on the farmers quite a bit, "because it's real life. The farmer will go out and spray exactly what the farmer would go out and spray. He's cost effective; he's not going to spray just because he wants to." Sanderson notes that the experiment station is an idealized, "too perfect" situation, and it benefits from the opportunity to see, through the work of the extension service and cooperating farmers, how their ideas and products actually perform in less controlled circumstances.

Martin Jager, who farmed the same forty acres for over sixty years, recalled an early experience with the extension service that illustrates this interplay between institutional sponsorship and vernacular agricultural literacy. After serving in WWII, Jager enrolled in agricultural vocational school; newly married, he was working the farm he inherited from his father, a piece of land on which he had practiced farming since he was a child. Jager was growing sweet bell peppers, a big cash crop in Samsula for many years. One of the agriculture courses was taught by a college graduate from another state, a literacy sponsor who "went by the book" and advised his students to improve their soil for better production. According to the institutional instruction, farmers needed to add dolomite to their soil, advice that was given on good faith but with little knowledge of Samsula's physical geology. The dolomite was freely delivered by truck and spread over the ground, but as Jager recalls, "from then on we never grew a bell pepper that was fit" to sell. The ground had been made "too sweet" (alkaline) for the peppers. Sixty-plus years after the event, the details are still vivid in his anecdote as a cautionary tale and a reflection on the multiple literacies that undergird successful farming. Presumably the extension service also learned from these kinds of experiences.

Sponsorship is thus a reciprocal process. Through the extension service, the agricultural literacies of the land-grant colleges and experiment stations may be introduced into the local community, but they are shaped in the process of application and adaptation. Farmers know their own land through experience, trial, error, and success; they test and try the new ideas and technologies, talk to each other, compare results, and reiterate lessons from the past, and then provide valuable feedback to the extension service. Bavec provided another example of how this might work when he noted that sometimes farmers would come up with their own chemical combinations, based on prior experience, to work against a pest or weed. As he pointed out, "of course the university couldn't do it because the label said they couldn't," but farmers might cautiously go around those constraints. Bavec explained to me that, if such an application was successful and the results were shared with the agent and vendor, eventually the chemical company would come out with a product that adopted the new combination. The agricultural literacy these farmers were practicing did not ignore the label because they could not read nor understand it, but because—from shared experience and acquired agricultural literacies—they felt confident in trying something new.

The Business of Farming: The Farm Record Book

As sponsors of agricultural literacy, the overall goal of the land-grant college, experiment stations, and extension service was to improve the viability of farming as a business. While many of my interviews revealed that farming can be an unpredictable business dependent on many variables not within the bounds of human control, archival texts from the extension service suggest that this uncertainty could be overcome if only farming was organized after the fashion of other industrial sectors. The 1939 *Annual Report of Work* describes one of the methods the extension service developed toward this end, a system to help the farmers keep track of "farm record work" (Nettles and Clayton 3).[11] W. T. Nettles, the District Agent, observes that in 1936 he and his team had "handled, summarized, and taken back to farmers 409 farm accounts and cost of production records covering citrus, poultry, potatoes and dairy work," and that they planned to use these records to help the grower understand "the weak as well as the strong points in his modus operandi" (3). The state account from 1939, the *Silver Anniversary Report*, describes the two record books that are part of the program as "one book ... intended for those who desire to keep detailed records by enterprises," and another "arranged for chronological entries only ... for monthly and annual summaries. It is intended for use on small farms ... " (27). The *Silver Anniversary Report* goes on to indicate that not only will the record books help the farmers using them, but they will provide data for longitudinal analysis on a broader scale (28).

Farm record books, in one form or another, were a part of the extension service from early in the program's existence.[12] A state report describes their successful implementation:

> Farm record books have been supplied to more than 2,000 farmers and assistance has been given to many of them in entering inventories and otherwise posting their books. Noted improvement has been made by farmers in their record keeping during 1944 as a result of their realization of the advantages to be obtained from accurate records when they compute income tax returns ... (*1944 Report* 24)

What is most interesting from the perspective of this research is how the language shifts and changes over time around the idea of farm record books, reflecting the different ways in which this genre generated and participated in literate activity. A genre arises in response to a recurring situation, so the implementation of formal record-keeping might indicate an inability or unwillingness of some members of the farming community to formally manage agricultural procedures.[13] At the same time, an equally compelling recurring situation might be the need of the extension service to have more visibility of the processes undergirding farm practices. From the comments about longitudinal observations in the *Silver Anniversary Report*, it seems clear that the extension service used the data acquired from these records for at least some tracking purposes of its own. If farmers kept detailed, verifiable records, the extension service would also have statistics to back up their claims of efficacy.

We can thus see the farm record book as an example of an intermediary genre that served the purposes of the literacy sponsor at least as much as it served the needs of the farmer. The record books affirm that the generative institutions—the USDA and the state extension service—were invested in the standardization and regimentation of farm production, as the introduction of the farm record book regularized both the processes of agriculture and the kinds of information that could be tracked. Farm record books, as data collection instruments, could be collected, analyzed, and quantified to show the changes taking place through progressive farm science techniques, thus ensuring a data-based assessment of agricultural progress and a validation of the extension service's value as a literacy sponsor.

In my Samsula research, Jager was the only interview participant who spoke of learning record-keeping from the extension service (in conjunction with his vocational agriculture classes in the 1940s), and he made light of the exercise. The "bookwork," from his perspective, did not take into account the vagaries of weather, insects, and other facts of farm life, and made no allowances for these effects on profit and loss situations. The other study participants (who took over family farms in the 1960s and after) did not make mention of farm ledgers or book-keeping, although they all spoke of running their farms as profit-generating businesses. In trying to understand what the records intimate as ubiquitous practice and the relative invisibility of farm record books at the local level, I came to believe that the practices of record-keeping might be entering the community through another route, one that could be explored by looking at a related adaptation in Samsula agricultural literacy: the connection between the extension service and community youth.

In both the interviews and extension service reports, the 4-H youth program stands out as a place where two cultures—the local community and the extension service—overlap and illuminate another contact zone. Two of the farmers I interviewed had been active in the 4-H as youths, and between their recollections and the information contained in the extension service documents a picture of literacy sponsorship, genre use, and practical learning comes into focus. The agricultural aspect of 4-H clubs brought the experience and formal knowledge of the extension service agent together with the young men who had an interest or a background in farming.[14] Nationalized in 1914 as part of the extension service, the 4-H has its roots in the boys and girls clubs organized at the beginning of the century ("4-H History"). Early mentions in the state reports categorize the clubs by livestock or vegetable, such as "Pig Club," "Calf Club," or "Corn Club" (*Annual Report, 1925* 28-29). The local agents oversaw and helped organize the clubs, and this work was seen as significant enough to the overall goals of the extension service that agents reported the time spent "devoted to club work" (*Silver Anniversary* 50). The 1918 state *Annual Report*, for example, shows that agents dedicated to boys' club work had equal status with the district agents and that the youth programs were considered "one of the most important features of the agent's activities" (27).

Local 4-H chapters not only interfaced with the county extension agents, but also with other 4-H clubs from across the district and across the state. Club members were brought together at annual recreational camps; short courses at the University of Florida (a land-grant college); county, regional, and state fairs, where they exhibited; and local, state, regional, and national competitions, where they vied for awards and recognition. The reasoning for the different events is spelled out in the reports, in which each activity is seen as contributing to the development of the individual and the organization. For example, the annual camps are seen as a social exercise and reward for work accomplished, and also as a way for "the county agent [to] hold his members from year to year" (*Annual Report, 1924* 43). Club members had certain criteria to meet in order to attend camp, as recorded in the 1954 Volusia County report, which notes that "fifty-six boys were selected to attend camp on the basis of meeting attendance, project work, and record books" (Townsend and Luttrell 7).

Short courses are another reward-based opportunity that exposed Samsula youths to agricultural literacies through the University of Florida. The 1925 state report describes the experience as thus:

> The winning boys in every county gather at the University. They receive practical instruction in agriculture but the greatest good derived is from the inspiration to go to college which gets hold of the boys ... Each year the number of former students that enter the University increases. All these boys do not enter the College of Agriculture; but better a successful lawyer or doctor than an uneducated, dissatisfied farmer. (30)

Boys could earn scholarships to the short courses from local civic organizations such as the Kiwanis and Lions Clubs, and business and government associations such as the Chambers of Commerce and Board of County Commissioners (Townsend and Luttrell, *Annual ... 1954* 7). In addition to the short courses, other incentives included scholarships and trips, awards supported by entities such as Amour & Co., which sponsored an annual trip to the Chicago International Live Stock Show; the Florida Banker's Association, which awarded scholarships to the Agricultural College (*Annual Report, 1924* 43); and the Sears-Roebuck Foundation, the State Department of Agriculture, and local feed stores, which contributed to prizes in the Dairy-Poultry Show at the county fair (Townsend and Luttrell, *Annual ... 1954* 8). These organizations and institutions, acting as literacy sponsors, saw the value of enculturating agricultural literacy in upcoming generations of potential farmers since these programs were also grooming future associates and customers.

All of the rewards were predicated on 4-H projects and their accompanying project books. While the earliest boys clubs only had a limited range of activities such as the corn club and the pig club, later programs expanded the breadth of subjects and interests. In 1955, for example, the *Annual Report of Volusia County* listed projects in "Corn, Irish Potatoes, Sweet Potatoes, gardening, poultry, citrus, goats, beef, swine, rabbits, bees, forestry, nursery, ornamentals and citrus, bulbs, farm and home electricity, farm and home safety, soil conservation and tractor maintenance" (Townsend and Luttrell 6). The boys were guided in these efforts by parents and by the agent or other representatives of the extension service. "Demonstrations and lessons in agricultural subjects" were given to groups, and the agent would also visit individual 4-H member's homes "to aid the club boys in carrying out the latest and best methods in agriculture" (Townsend and Luttrell 6). In 1955, these efforts in Volusia County resulted in 421 completed projects by 232 club members (6).

In the mention of "latest and best methods in agriculture," we hear the continuing drumbeat of progressive farm practices. As in their work with adult farmers, the extension agents used a variety of methods to inculcate these ideas and practices, such as live demonstrations and workshops. Additionally, 4-H members were encouraged to compete, individually and in teams, with each other. Project competitions could take the form of demonstration, such as the tractor-driving competition in which Vadnal participated in 1954, or showing a prize pig at the county fair. Competitions could also affirm the protocols of USDA programs. Bavec remembered learning how to grade vegetables in a 4-H competition, a skill that he carried into his adult farming experience. He related that "they started the vegetable judging team, when I was one of the older members in the 4-H club … you had to identify weeds, you had to identify diseases, you had to identify all the varieties, different varieties of cucumbers, cabbage, carrots, peppers."

When asked to describe the process, Bavec remembered working in a team and filling in a form, like a test sheet. This genre guided the participants through the produce judging process:

> You go to the state contest and they've got a cabbage plant here with black rot, and it's A, B, C, and D, and one of them is black rot and that's the one you check, then you go to the next area and they have a crabgrass and you go there and it may be a fill in the blank: this is "crabgrass," and you go to the next one, and there would be three cucumbers. And the first one is straight, the next one is crooked, and this one's got a … yeah, a little bit of decay on it, and you had to give it a grade, just like the federal standards of grading produce.

While his team did not place first, the experience gave Bavec a feeling of authority on the subject. As a retired farmer, he jokes that he felt confident around the federal inspectors because of his 4-H knowledge, and he would tell them "if you don't judge my produce right, I'm going to appeal it, you know, because I know enough." Whether or not the sponsors in this case intended to give those they sponsored the confidence to challenge USDA decisions is debatable, but the outcome of the literacy gains from 4-H coupled with Bavec's experience in the farming community had that effect.

Young people in 4-H selected projects from the available choices, and then track of everything that was associated with the project in a record book. One research participant remembered a turkey project that he undertook in 4-H over sixty years ago. While some of the details were lost to time, he remembered that the birds were "Bronze Wagonwheel strain" and that he heard "the grandfather, if there's such a thing for turkeys, weighed in excess of 60 lbs." He also recalled that he had to keep records on them, "feed, and medications, the initial cost," a chore his father helped him with since he had "never been tasked to do something like that before." The knowledge gained through projects such as this was experiential, but part of that experience was assimilating the specific literacies needed for keeping a record book. Exposure to the 4-H project record book was immersion in the kinds of information the extension service valued, and the types of genres necessary for the business of agriculture.

While the 4-H project record and the farm record book might respond to different rhetorical situations, they are genetically related in origin and purpose. The project record genre is an introductory text, with simplified ledgers and self-reflective pages; it provides the rationale for record-keeping, such as "To train yourself for future work" (*4-H Project* 2). It also asks for goals—at the start of the project—and things learned—at the end of the project; these self-reflective sections help the project owner develop meta-awareness of the process they are going through. The short ledger section is patterned on actual farm ledgers, but simplified for the beginning entrepreneur. For the extension service sponsors, the goal was to get young people thinking in terms of costs and benefits and organizing those thoughts on paper. The ideas and values of modern farm production thus entered the experience and helped shape the perceptions of young 4-H participants. The information they recorded in their project records helped fulfill project work, but it also shaped their agricultural literacies for adult farming pursuits.

As a genre in the rhetorical overlap between the Samsula agricultural community and the extension service, the project record brought the "new" knowledge the young people learned in their 4-H activities together with their community farming experiences. For someone like Bavec, who grew up around truck farming, learning the formal aspects of judging vegetables in 4-H gave him the confidence to speak with authority when he marketed his own produce as an adult. Vadnal completed many projects and had opportunities to attend short courses at the University of Florida. In 1954, he won the state Farm and Home Safety Award Program; he also won the state Tractor Driving Contest, for which he received a gold watch and a chance to compete in the Atlantic States Operators Contest in Richmond, Virginia (Townsend and Luttrell 8). In 1955, he received a county award in leadership (Townsend and Luttrell 7), and in 1956 he served as an officer on the 4-H leadership council. While he has farmed as an adult, his primary vocation, as stated during his interview, is Certified Public Accountant. Vadnal does not attribute his career to his experience in 4-H, but it does seem that the kind of exposure to process and organization facilitated by 4-H project work is a good foundation for a career in accounting.

Confidence, organization, and other leadership qualities are results of the transitional literacies 4-H members experienced. The literate skills they gained from 4-H were not in opposition to the community dialogues and understandings with which they grew up, but were structured in a way that supported the goals of the extension service and all the literacy sponsors with which it aligns: the experiment stations, the land-grant college, and the USDA. In addition, other corporate and civic sponsors had access to these young people through systems of incentives and awards, subtly establishing future relationships. The ideologies brought to bear by these sponsors, like the processes inculcated through the project record, are not always visible, even if they are always shaping perceptions of modern American agriculture.

Combined with the archival materials from the extension service, the narratives provided by the local farmers of Samsula provide insight into the responsive nature of agricultural literacy sponsorship. This research depicts the ways in which sponsorship is a recursive process, as local farmers who employed institutional knowledge were contributing to, as well as assimilating, the new ideas, methods, and technologies of twentieth-century agriculture. While much research remains to be done in this area, this study shows that the extension service, and in particular the 4-H youth clubs, promoted agricultural literacies which reinforced USDA guidelines of what premium quality vegetables look like and how they should be grown, and in the process influenced new generations of agriculturalists. Institutional pressures to manage farming as a predictable business, as revealed in the farm record book initiatives, would in time translate to the factory farming practices of the current era, leaving small-scale truck farmers unable to compete in large markets. Instead, the farmers who survived at this level of agriculture, such as several of my interview subjects, found new customers in farmer's markets and roadside stands. Understanding the milieu out of which these produce vendors came, and the agricultural literacies that influenced them, can in turn help us understand some of our own expectations and preferences—our own food literacies—when we look at fresh vegetables in the produce aisle.

Endnotes

1. "Truck farming" describes moderate-sized operations—10-20 acres—that might grow a variety of crops.

2. Brewster defines agricultural literacy as "a functional literacy characterized by the acquisition of knowledge and skills required to perform in particular contexts or to assist sponsoring agencies in achieving particular aims" (36-37).

3. For a description of significant agricultural legislation that set the stage for agricultural knowledge to become a formalized sphere for technical and scientific inquiry in the United States, see Cresap 220-224.

4. I will use fictitious names for all interview participants in this paper.

5. See Brewster 36-37 for a discussion of organizations and institutions contributing to modern agricultural literacies.

6. The 1909 *Report of the Country Life Commission*, initiated by President Theodore Roosevelt, stressed that "the business of agriculture must be made to yield a reasonable return to those who follow it intelligently, and life on the farm must be made permanently satisfying to intelligent, progressive people" (17).

7. The idea of multiple literacies in this study aligns with Brandt's perspective of literacy sponsors working in and responding to specific, local situations. See also Barton for a discussion on interconnected communities and the various literacies at work within and between them.

8. For an explanation of contact zones as areas of cross-cultural dynamics and fluid boundaries, see Pratt 35-37.

9. Brandt argues that literacy sponsors and those they sponsor share a "reciprocal relationship" (167).

10. See Brown and Duguid's perspective of collective knowledge in *The Social Life of Information* (103).

11. The material analyzed for this research (texts spanning dates from 1915 to 1970) comes from archival extension service reports housed in the University of Florida Special and Area Collections and available in University of Florida Digital Collections.

12. An example of a blank 1934 farm record book can be seen at the *HathiTrust Digital Library*.

13. This view of genre poses genre texts as social responses to recurring rhetorical situations. See Miller's 1984 article "Genre as Social Action"; also Bazerman and Devitt. As social responses, genres can also help us discern a community's "norms, epistemology, ideology, and social ontology" (Berkenkotter and Huckin 497).

14. While some young women engaged in the agricultural aspects of 4-H, most were channeled into what was at the time considered "woman's work" in projects such as canning, sewing, and home management. This was reflective of the sexual dichotomies persistent in the culture of the times, and not the abilities or proclivities of the participants. For the purposes of this paper, references to 4-H projects and rewards focus on boys' work.

Works Cited

1944 Report, Florida Agricultural Extension Service. Agricultural Extension Service, U of Florida. Gainesville, 1944. *ufdc.ufl.edu*. Web. 12 Jan. 2014.
"4-H History." *About 4-H*. National 4-H Council. *4-h.org*. Web. 6 Aug. 2014.
"4-H Project Record." U of Florida Cooperative Extension Service. 1985. *ufdc.ufl.edu*. Web. 7 Aug. 2014.
Annual Report, 1918: Report of General Activities for 1918. U of Florida Division of Agricultural Extension and USDA Cooperating. Gainesville, 1919. Google Books. Web. 14 July 2014.
Annual Report, 1924: Report of General Activities for 1924. Agricultural Extension Service, U of Florida, Florida State College for Women, and USDA. Gainesville, 1924. Google Books. Web. 14 July 2014.
Annual Report, 1925: Report of General Activities for 1925. Agricultural Extension Service, U of Florida, Florida State College for Women, and USDA. Gainesville, 1925. Google Books. Web. 14 July 2014.

Barton, David. "Literacy Practices in Local Activities: An Ecological Approach." *Ecological Education in Everyday Life: ALPHA 2000*. Ed. Jean-Paul Hautecoeur. Toronto: U of Toronto P, 2002. 137-49. Print.

Bazerman, Charles. "Speech Acts, Genres, and Activity Systems: How Texts Organize Activity and People." *What Writing Does and How It Does It: An Introduction to Analyzing Texts and Textual Practices*. Ed. Bazerman and Paul A. Prior. Mahwah: Lawrence Erlbaum, 2004. 309-39. Print.

Berkenkotter, Carol and Thomas N. Huckin. "Rethinking Genre from a Sociocognitive Perspective." *Written Communication* 10.4 (1993): 475-509. SAGE. Web. 10 Apr. 2014.

Brandt, Deborah. "Sponsors of Literacy." *College Composition and Communication* 49.2 (1998) 165-185. NCTE. Web. 26 May 2012.

Brewster, Cori. "Toward a Critical Agricultural Literacy." *Reclaiming the Rural: Essays on Literacy, Rhetoric, and Pedagogy*. Ed. Kim Donehower, Charlotte Hogg, and Eileen E. Schell. Carbondale: Southern Illinois UP, 2012. 34-51. Print.

Brown, John Seely and Paul Duguid. *The Social Life of Information*. Boston: Harvard Business School P, 2000. Print.

Cresap, Ida Keeling. *The History of Florida Agriculture: The Early Era*. Ed. Hervey Sharpe. Gainesville, 1982. *Ufdc.ufl.edu*. Web. 21 Jan. 2012.

Devitt, Amy J. "An Analysis of Genres in Social Settings." *Writing Genres*. Carbondale: Southern Illinois UP, 2004. 33-65. Print.

Farm Record Book. USDA. Washington, DC: 1934. *HathiTrust Digital Library*. Web. 30 July 2014.

Miller, Carolyn. "Genre as Social Action." *Quarterly Journal of Speech* 70 (1984): 151-67. *MLA International Bibliography*. Web. 1 June 2012.

Nettles, W. T. and H. G. Clayton. *Annual Report of Work, Central and Southern Florida, 1939*. Agricultural Extension Service, U of Florida. Series 91, Subseries 91a, Box 1. Annual Reports of the Florida Cooperative Extension Service, Special and Area Studies Collections, George A. Smathers Libraries, U of Florida, Gainesville, FL. 3 March 2014.

Nettles, W. T. *District and Leader Reports, 1936*. Agricultural Extension Service, U of Florida. Series 91, Subseries 91a, Box 1. Annual Reports of the Florida Cooperative Extension Service, Special and Area Studies Collections, George A. Smathers Libraries, U of Florida, Gainesville, FL. 3 March 2014.

Pratt, Mary Louise. "Arts of the Contact Zone." *Profession* (1991): 33-40. *JSTOR*. Web. 26 Aug. 2012.

Report of the Country Life Commission. Washington: GPO, 1909. Harvard College Library Theodore Roosevelt Collection. Google Books. Web. 12 June 2014. PDF file.

Silver Anniversary Report, Florida Agricultural Extension Service Annual Report 1939. Agricultural Extension Service, U of Florida, Florida State College for Women, and USDA. Gainesville: The Service, 1939. *Ufdc.ufl.edu*. Web. 12 Jan. 2014.

Townsend, T. R. and James N. Luttrell. *Annual Report of Volusia County: 1954*. Series 91, Subseries 91b, Box 26. Annual Reports of the Florida Cooperative Extension Service, Special and Area Studies Collections, George Smathers Libraries, U of Florida, Gainesville, FL. 3 March 2014.

———. *Annual Report of Volusia County: 1955*. Series 91, Subseries 91b, Box 31. Annual Reports of the Florida Cooperative Extension Service, Special and Area Studies Collections, George Smathers Libraries, U of Florida, Gainesville, FL. 3 March 2014.

Author Bio

Marcy L. Galbreath received her PhD in Texts & Technology from the University of Central Florida in 2014, and is currently a lecturer in UCF's Department of Writing and Rhetoric. Her research focuses on the rhetoric of science in relation to agricultural and environmental communications, how these communications are enacted in oral, print, and digital genres, and how the literacies associated with these genres contribute to meaning-making within and between associated communities.

Community Cookbooks: Sponsors of Literacy and Community Identity

Lisa Mastrangelo

This article looks at the various ways that communities can be "read" through their cookbooks. Recipes and collections can reveal much about communities, including shared memories/traditions, geographical identifications, and representations of class.

"[Recipes] take the ingredients of history, class, region, theology, identity, and family and from them fashion new and continuing systems of community" (Ferguson 713).

Last summer, as part of a decision to organize my kitchen, I sorted my cookbooks. Much to my surprise, I realized that I was in possession of multiple community cookbooks from various communities that at some point had been a part of my life—cookbooks produced by certain groups of people who were understood to share common characteristics or interests. As Marion Nestle notes in her introduction to *Books that Cook*, cookbooks and recipes tell stories, both about food and about the locations where and conditions under which they were produced. "They convey myths. They are replete with drama, symbolic meaning, and psychological insight. Furthermore, they offer plenty to talk about: culture, religion, ethics, personal identity, and anything else it means to be human" (xvi). This is even truer of community cookbooks, which often reveal nuances about those communities and their self-representations.

What started as a general interest in reading my own past and experiences quickly led me to see the value of these cookbooks as rhetorical artifacts that reveal much about their communities. These cookbooks function as literate practices of a community, sponsored by the community members who were themselves cooks, contributors, readers, organizers and editors. As Deborah Brandt notes in "Sponsors of Literacy," such sponsors are "any agents, local or distant, concrete or abstract, who enable, support, teach, model, as well as recruit, regulate, suppress, or withhold literacy—and gain advantage by it in some way" (166). Those who produce these cookbooks, then, gain advantage by the sale of the cookbooks themselves, but also offer outside readers context clues for understanding their communities. As such, the cookbooks function as "alternative public spaces," where "ordinary people develop public voices, letting us characterize the distinctive features of these discursive spaces, [and] the discourses they circulate" (Higgins, Long, and Flower 10). Indeed, through their publication they create a snapshot of their communities, a picture and reflection of who they are and who they want people to think that they might be. Through this lens, this article will explore key identities of the communities represented in the cookbooks, including shared memories and traditions, geographical identifications, and representations of class.

Background and Organization

Because of the diversity of their representations, I chose to explore two of the cookbooks in my collection: *Bouquet Garni*, a cookbook produced by the alumnae of Mount Holyoke College, of which I am one, and published in 1978 and 1986, and *76: The Bicentennial Cookbook of the Senior Citizens of Maine and Newark Valley*. *Bouquet Garni* was created by and sold by and to alumnae of Mount Holyoke College, a large group of culturally and geographically diverse women of a wide age-range, although fairly homogenously middle-to-upper class and mostly white at this time.[1] The *76* cookbook was produced by the residents of the towns of Newark Valley and Maine, New York, and was widely distributed in and around those towns—I received a copy as the grandniece of one of the residents of Newark Valley. These residents were local and not widespread, and were more restricted in age—all senior citizens as of 1976. In addition, the residents of Maine and Newark Valley at this time were largely working class and almost entirely white.[2]

Like most community cookbooks, neither *Bouquet Garni* nor *76* has a single author or a single voice, but rather a hidden, mostly anonymous group of sponsors. Alison Kelly notes that in this respect community cookbooks are different from other cookbooks—they are created by groups of nonprofessionals. As a result, the reader is not always sure who is talking throughout the books, or what the books assume about their listeners (43). Because the sponsorship of such work is sometimes hidden, readers come to the cookbooks with varying degrees of understanding of the representations presented by the texts, but an overall sense that these are communal "memory texts." As Rosalyn Collings Eves notes in "A Recipe for Remembrance: Memory and Identity in African-American Women's Cookbooks," cookbooks work to "memorialize both individuals and community, to invoke 'memory beyond mind,' and to generate a sense of collective memory that in turn shapes communal identity" (281). They are literate practices steeped in the communal memories of the sponsors that produced them. These two particular cookbooks are particularly strong examples that show the ways that in-depth readings of the community cookbooks can make the situatedness of the cookbooks more visible.[3]

What does it mean to be a literate reader of these recipes, one who can decipher greater meanings about the community through an understanding of the work of the sponsors of the cookbooks? As Eves notes, it is to understand the "narrative framework around which memories, both individual and communal, are constructed and invested with meaning" (282). It means to read the recipes and the collections—their social, textual, geographical, and historical clues—in order to garner a greater understanding of the meaning of the texts. The greater the understanding on the part of the reader, the greater their participation in the community.

Both of the cookbooks have unique features in their organization and presentation. *Bouquet Garni* (see Figure 1), for example, is professionally printed and bound, with a white and green plastic cover designed by an alumna from the Class of 1975. Within the first few pages, the reader finds the subtitle "A liberal sample for the fine art of cooking from alumnae of Mount Holyoke College" in addition to a brief description of the college's history and location.

Figure 1: Bouquet Garni cookbook

The collection begins with an introduction provided by an anonymous "Bouquet Garni Committee," who thank the alumnae from around the world who shared their recipes. The Committee also provides an intriguing piece of information about the fact that they had tested each and every recipe themselves before including it. In general, the cookbooks that I looked at do not offer a sense for this type of involvement, but assume that the contributor is trustworthy and has tested the recipe themselves for accuracy and edibility. Thus, the *Bouquet Garni* committee had already created a relationship with the recipes before passing them to the reader, cooking and eating each recipe included and inviting the readers to join the community by doing the same.

76: The Bicentennial Cookbook of the Senior Citizens of Maine and Newark Valley contrasts greatly to *Bouquet Garni*. It is much less formal, and yet, seems more joyful. *76* is what Leonardi identifies as "a circle of enthusiastic and helpful friends reproduc[ing] the social context of recipe sharing" (342). The book itself is hand-typed and then reproduced (see Figure 2); there are no page numbers, nor is there an index. The book starts with a tribute page to the volunteers and lists both the committee and the staff of "solicitors and typists" by name.

Figure 2: 76 cookbook

Unlike *Bouquet Garni*, whose sponsors organized the recipes in order of a meal—appetizers, vegetables, meats, and then desserts—*76* is organized by section, but the sections are organized alphabetically. Casseroles are listed just before Cookies, although the section on Desserts has headings to distinguish puddings, candy, and general desserts. Chicken recipes appear in the section on Fowl.

While the recipe organization may be different for most readers, so too may be the presence of advertising through the *76* cookbook. It is possible to gain a greater understanding about Maine and Newark Valley from the advertisements included in the book. While the beginning features only one ad from The Newark Valley Bank, there are approximately 20 pages of ads at the end of the book, including everything from Town and Country Electric to Croft's Trailer Hitches—"Get Properly Hitched at Crofts!" One understands from the ads that these towns are both small and close-knit.[4] The ads reflect a small-town sense of community with a focus on farming and agricultural industry. Ads are for excavators, industrial supply corporations, butchers, septic tanks, horse tractors, restaurants, and finally, the funeral home. Some ads include a small note; "Our Best Wishes to the Senior Citizens!" appears to be hand-drawn into the McKilligan Industrial Supply Corp. ad. Likewise, the editors of the cookbook speak back to their audience in thanks to their contributors: "Patronize our Advertisers" appears in more than one place in the ad section and likewise throughout the cookbook on nearly every other page. Readers here do not have to supply much context either for the recipes included or for the town; because of the extra materials included the reader is able to see more clearly the community's self-definition. The reader knows, upon entering the text, what kinds of places Maine and Newark Valley are, the ages of the contributors and organizers of the cookbook, and the types of eating they engaged in. While we may not know the individual stories of contributors, we can see their shared community and come to understand their cultural values and historical experiences through advertising as well as their food memories (Heck 205).

History and Traditions

The Mount Holyoke cookbook, *Bouquet Garni*, very clearly offers some context for the reader about the community it describes, but also assumes that the readers are familiar with the college's history and traditions (including their recipe and food traditions). A "community literacy" at work here is assumed; readers must provide their own knowledge of the college in order to fully understand the materials. The assumption exists that the readers are part of the same community as the sponsors and that they have in-depth knowledge regarding the world of Mount Holyoke.

There is an overall sense for the reader of *Bouquet Garni* that the Mount Holyoke community of women is defined by the recipes as a prominent one. The first recipe in the Desserts section, for example, is "Governor Ella Grasso's Seven-Layer Cake." There is no other mention about the fact that Ella Grasso was the first female governor of Connecticut, but there is a definite understanding that this is an important recipe. It takes the first spot in the Cakes section of the Desserts chapter, and is of course labeled with the fact that it was the Governor's contribution. Perhaps the most famous contributor in the cookbook, however, is poet Emily Dickinson, who surely did not know she was contributing. The introduction mentions her recipe as a traditional one—although the origin of the recipe is not given—and the recipe itself has more commentary than most, noting "This specialty of Emily Dickinson (who attended Mount Holyoke in 1848), was made famous by Julie Harris who portrayed the poet in [the play] 'The Belle of Amherst'" (200). As part of the culture and traditions of Mount Holyoke, it likely would be difficult to find an alumna who could not name

Dickinson as one of the more famous students of the institution. The inclusion of Grasso and Dickinson reminds readers that the community self-defines as prominent. But the inclusion of such figures also reinforces memories of the traditions that Mount Holyoke holds as important.

While famous people are represented in *Bouquet Garni*, the sponsors of 76 also participate in the inclusion of such "important" recipes. The very first two recipes in 76 stand alone and are for Baked Turkey Casserole and New York State Apple Pie. However, the reader immediately understands the implications of this since the first recipe is accompanied by a letter from Marba S. Perrott, Director of Correspondence for Mrs. Ford, wife of United States President Gerald Ford. The letter indicates that the Turkey Casserole Recipe is from the White House files of "First Family" recipes, and Perrott wishes the seniors the best of luck with their fundraising. The second recipe is submitted by Elizabeth Maher on behalf of Mrs. Rockefeller and the Office of the Vice President. Rockefeller was originally from New York State, and so the recipe for New York State Apple Pie is particularly fitting. The inclusion of both recipes shows the ways in which the citizens of Newark Valley and Maine define themselves as part of a larger, national community at the same time that they celebrate their own small towns.

Perhaps the recipe that most carefully represents a community and its traditions, however, is the recipe for Deacon Porter's Hat in *Bouquet Garni*. Deacon Porter's Hat is a dense brown bread-like steamed pudding, typically served with a hard sauce. It is a traditional dessert on the campus despite the fact that very few students actually like it—I speak from experience. Next to the recipe for Deacon Porter's Hat in the cookbook is the vague "A traditional dessert at Mount Holyoke," and most alumnae could tell you that it exists and know some variation of the story surrounding it, even if they have not been brave enough to try it. Its story appears in Frances Lester Warner's 1937 *On a New England Campus*. Warner describes the history of Deacon Porter's Hat's name as existing "because its shape reminded the early students of the tall hat worn by our first Trustee in Charge of Building" (Warner)[5]. There is little context given for the recipe in *Bouquet Garni*, but the assumption of the sponsors of the cookbook is that the reader who might pick up *Bouquet Garni* (and a recipe like "Deacon Porter's Hat") will likely have some association with the college community and therefore be able to participate in the community created by the recipe, even if she could not remember the actual story behind it. According to Elizabeth Fleitz's "Cooking Codes: Cookbook Discourse as Women's Rhetorical Practices," the combination of social, textual, and embodied practices that readers bring to a cookbook like *Bouquet Garni* provide "hints on how to interpret the discourse and 'crack' the code, thus leading to a fuller understanding of the cultural and rhetorical significance of the text" (6). Thus, women's experiences of spending four years being served Deacon Porter's Hat, in a particular place at a particular time, rhetorically codes the recipe for the participants of that experience and thus most readers of the cookbook. Alumnae readers, therefore, are able to engage dialectically with the recipe, identifying themselves clearly as literate members of the defined community.[6]

The recipe for Deacon Porter's Hat also rhetorically functions to encourage both participation and remembrance in the community. If alums cannot be a part of the Mount Holyoke Community physically, they can still participate in the traditions of the institution from their own homes, and contribute to their literate involvement in this way. As Eves note, "because cookbooks encourage interaction, consumption, and embodiment, they may also encourage active remembrance" (287). Participating in the recipes of the community, then, becomes a way to remain connected to the dialogue and continue to participate in the community.[7]

Geographic Representations

In addition to locating the communities historically/traditionally, many of the recipes in both collections also reflect their sense of geography. In *Bouquet Garni*, for example, the contribution of international recipes reminds readers that they are also participating in a community that is both socially diverse and literate in the cuisine of other cultures and regions. In the Introduction, the editors make it clear that they sought a "rich mix of cuisines" for the cookbook, including those from a wide range of geographical areas in the United States as well as those from around the world. "She Crab Soup from Alabama, and Baked Whole Salmon from the northwest mingle appetizingly with Iranian Lamb, Tandoori Chicken, and Carbonada Criolla, a Farmer's Stew from Argentina." Some context is provided within the cookbook for such recipes as well. The recipe for Nigerian Meatballs, for example, has the comment "peanuts are a major source of protein in Africa," and the recipe for Pescado En Escabeche is labeled "A pickled fish dish from Puerto Rico" (10-11). While there is not necessarily a sense for where the recipes came from—that part of the self-identification is missing from the Nigerian Meatballs recipe, and the contributor is listed as being from Boston, Massachusetts—sometimes the context is more obvious. The contributor of the recipe for the traditional Puerto Rican fish dish, for example, lists herself as a resident of Puerto Rico. These outward and visible inclusions help readers understand the ways in which the contributors are situated.

76, in contrast, shows the regional locality of Western New York State in 1976. The names in the collection are typical western New York senior citizen names from 1976—Agnes, Elsie, Trudy, Eunice, Harold, and Milton are all thanked in the list of solicitors. Last names such as Hutchings, Stimming, Eastman, Murch, and Hart all indicate a Western European origin for the families contributing to the cookbook—primarily English, with some French and German origins. Kelly makes an interesting note about the names of cookbook contributors, commenting that they are "a path to discovering more about the cultural context of any given community cookbook," and this is certainly visible in the *76*(41).

Geographical self-definitions are further expressed in *76* with the inclusion of recipes for local dishes that western New Yorkers would find familiar but others might find a-contextual. A recipe for *spiedies*, a marinated, grilled type of meat still commonly eaten in the area, is included. According to local lore, the spiedie was brought to the area by Italian immigrants and the recipe is supposed to be a closely guarded secret

("Eating History"). Traditionally, spiedies were made from lamb, although now they are more commonly made from pork or chicken. Locals looking in the cookbook, however, would have been well acquainted with them as a local food, as, indeed, they still are today. Recognition of the importance of such local and regional recipes creates what Ferguson calls "autochthony," a sense of something originating from or being formed in a particular place (712). Much like the recipe for Deacon Porter's Hat, while a person who was not literate to this community might not recognize the importance of the inclusion of the spiedies recipe, informed readers of the cookbook most certainly would.

Likewise, readers might actually gain some knowledge about the local area through certain recipes included by the sponsors. For example, there is a lengthy section in 76 on making preserves from produce that would have been abundantly and locally available (zucchini marmalade and crab apple, strawberry, and rhubarb jellies all appear alongside multiple recipes for pickles). The context here is one for locals—much as locals would know about spiedies, they would also know which ingredients (fruits and vegetables in particular) were available seasonally to complete the recipes. Such inclusions are typical of community cookbooks, which Ferguson notes often define their regionality through such recipes as "sauces, vinegars, or jams" (711), at a point in time when canning and food preservation were important tools for survival.

The 76 cookbook sponsors also reflect small town USA when they intersperse the recipes with songs, prayers, aphorisms and poems throughout the book. In the Meat section, for example, the recipe for "Happy Day" appears, contributed by Agnes Perry of Maine: "Take a pinch of patience, 'folks,' mix with work and fun. Stir awhile and add a smile for that's the way it's done. Pepper up the lot with pluck, serve the best you may. There's no foolproof recipe for a happy day." The sponsors' inclusion of "extra" materials signifies a community that wants to reflect itself as value driven and close-knit (see Figure 3).

Figure 3: Recipe for Ham and Noodle Casserole with an aphorism underneath it. Also note the "Patronize our Advertisers."

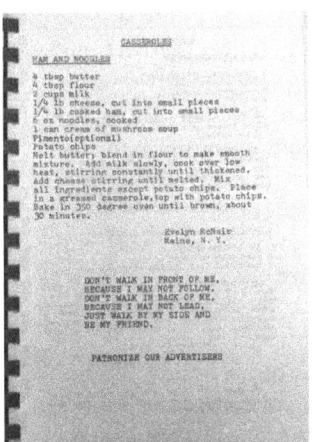

Much the way that Deacon Porter's Hat does this in *Bouquet Garni*, the "extras" create a sense of togetherness and belonging throughout the cookbook. As Eves says, "they generate a sense of *collective* memory," creating an extended dinner table that includes the entire community, even if members are not physically present at that given moment (293).

Rhetorically, the geographical and local elements in both cookbooks create what Eves defines as a "memorial text." As she notes, "as memorial texts, the stories inscribed in these cookbooks are both static and dynamic—static in their moment of inscription, but dynamic in the way they add to and help shape broader communal narratives and memories" (287).

There is a clear sense of the community that is signified within the recipes and this creates a stronger sense for who and what that community is. Using Eves' definition, the collections of recipes contain embedded discourse, that which creates "an exchange between a giver and a receiver, as well as exigence and context" (282), creating stronger community self-definitions.

Recipes as Indicators of Class Status

Perhaps one of the most interesting features of these two community cookbooks was the way in which they reflect class issues. Understanding the ways that class is represented in the recipes, closely examined, can help readers become more knowledgeable readers and interpreters of the community. As Eves notes, "we signal our group affiliation through food choices," creating "a powerful form of community identification" (288). Ferguson echoes this when he identifies community cookbooks as a location and space that "create and reinforce various class boundaries, both in their purpose and in their instruction" (706). Recipe choices made by the sponsors, then, can mark both group identity and cultural participation.

Even the titles of each volume can signify the community and the class expectations of the discourse inside. *Bouquet Garni*, which literally translates to "the garnished bouquet," is also the bundle of herbs, tied together, that is typically used to prepare soups, stocks, or the "base" elements of other dishes. With the 1961 (Volume 1) and 1970 (Volume 2) publications of Julia Child, Simone Beck, and Louisette Bertholle's *Mastering the Art of French Cooking*, the sponsors of *Bouquet Garni* would have understood the reference to French cooking—the bouquet garni is featured in many of the Child, Beck, and Bertholle recipes. The *Bouquet Garni* title signifies cosmopolitanism and upper class aspirations.

Conversely, the cover of *76: The Bicentennial Cookbook* reflects the patriotism of small-town America but does not overtly reflect class. The cover itself is red, white, and blue, and the flag on the cover with the "76" embedded in the original 13 star flag, with a fuller star flag in the background, reflects the community's sense of history and their participation in the larger national celebrations of that year. In this way, *76* broadcasts its participation in a larger national conversation.

The contents of each cookbook also send readers strong messages about class and class participation. The *Bouquet Garni* committee as sponsor, for example, includes a brief introduction to each section, and the reader immediately has the sense that food, in this context, has a purpose and a status. These are not common recipes meant simply for consumption of food or random recipes thrown together with minimal organization, as sometimes seems the case with *76*. Rather, these are instructions for cultured meals to be presented to and shared with others. The "Desserts" section, for example, starts with "Desserts are the final compliment to a well planned menu. If you have included a pastry such as a quiche or a phyllo dough recipe as part of your main course, offer a soft pudding; or Bavarian type dessert; if your meal has been rich or spicy, end it with a refreshing sherbet; a mousse or soufflé entrée or accompaniment can be balanced with a cake or fruit pie" (192). Such an introduction allows the reader to understand the context and purpose of the recipes. Food is defined here as a reflection of culture, and not merely an object for consumption.

The recipes in *Bouquet Garni* also imply that readers do not want or need budget-friendly recipes. *Bouquet Garni* contains no recipes that include industrially produced or heavily processed items, such as canned soups or meats/fish, Spam, or Jello-O, although gelatin is used for molded salad recipes. There are, however, recipes that reflect a predilection for "show" and entertainment such as the Ham Mousse Madeira—"Pink and pretty for a buffet"(93)—and the Chicken Soufflé Sandwich—"A sandwich baked in eggs and milk is so easy to do ahead for guests" (112). Both the soufflés and the molded salads were meant for appearance, and were popular "'dainty' creations" (Kelly 47).

Many of the recipes also reflect particular tastes during particular times, especially in meat. By the early 1900s, regular consumption of meat was considered a sign of wealth and prosperity, particularly for immigrants (Ziegelman 177). This is clearly reflected in *Bouquet Garni*. Most recipes call for fresh meats and fish and reflect a variety of types. For example, recipes for sweetbreads, venison, tongue, and roast pheasant point towards a time period when people regularly ate a greater variety of meats than currently are typically consumed.

Unlike *Bouquet Garni*, the recipes in *76* are not recipes for people who want to entertain and impress others. These are recipes for people who want to *eat* and want and need to be both thrifty and efficient while going about the process. Levi-Strauss calls this the difference between "'endo-cuisine' prepared for domestic use, destined to a small closed group," vs. "'exo-cuisine,' that which one offers to guests" (30). The recipes in *Bouquet Garni*, for example, are clearly meant for entertaining guests in the home. Conversely, the recipes in *76* are meant for consumption—to feed hungry family members nourishing food. This interior vs. exterior depiction of food also reinforces a class divide between the two cookbooks. In *76*, frugality and class issues are wholly visible in the recipes, and offer a glimpse into 1976 small-town Western New York. Multiple recipes, for example, call for processed and industrialized foods such as canned vegetables, cream of "x" soups (lots of cheddar cheese and mushroom, crushed corn flakes, margarine, Jell-O, cake mixes, hot dogs, Tang, and even Spam) my favorite is the recipe for Spam Casserole, which not only includes Spam but cream of cheddar soup. As Jennifer Wallach points out in *How America Eats*, such recipes reflect the introduction of industrialized food production around World War II and recipes that were created to serve cooks who lived through that time period. Women could be seen as "cooking" even as they were using industrially produced food products to save themselves time and money in the kitchen (139).[8] The recipes in *76* reflect the increased access to cheaper processed food that allowed cooks to both "stretch" recipes and cook food in less time.

The recipes that include such ingredients as Spam and Jell-O also reflect the conflicted class assumptions of the time period and location. As George H. Lewis notes in "From Minnesota Fat to Seoul Food: Spam in America and the Pacific Rim," the introduction of Spam, originally "invented" and produced in New York State, into American culture in 1937 afforded those who were not able to purchase fresh meats the ability to still consume meat. During World War II, citizens were encouraged to consume canned meats in order to assist the war effort and display patriotism (Lewis). Local communities such as Newark Valley took pride in their ability to contribute to the war effort and continued to use products such as Spam long after the war. At the same time that the 1976 publication of *76* was meant to celebrate the nation's bicentennial, Spam had also become both a symbol of pride and embarrassment for the nation. According to Lewis, by the 1980s (and certainly even by 1976) "most Americans had come to connect Spam symbolically to an earlier time of innocent-but-hokey pride and patriotism—something to be collectively embarrassed about but, at the same time, secretly prideful" (Lewis). Spam was celebrated in this sense by small-town Americans at the same time that a good deal of the rest of the world generally saw it as low-class. The senior residents of Newark Valley, who would have lived through the Depression and World War II, though, would have viewed Spam as both frugal and patriotic, and its inclusion in the cookbook is therefore not a surprise.

Much like the story of Spam, residents of Newark Valley and Maine may have been familiar with the LeRoy, New York roots of Jell-O, which is also a defining ingredient in the cookbook. Their inclusion of recipes with Jell-O would, much like their inclusion of Spam recipes, harkened back to World War II, when citizens were encouraged to use Jell-O as part of a meatless, wheat-free diet. As Katherine LeBesco notes in "There's Always Room for Resistance: Jell-O, Gender, and Social Class," Jell-O has long been used to extend meals and to produce dessert on a budget. However, it has also come to be associated with lower social class (141). *Bouquet Garni,* in contrast to *76,* only includes one recipe that contains gelatin (not Jell-O per se), which is the molded Ham Mousse Madeira. Conversely, the *76* includes six recipes for Jell-O salads, including two basic Jell-O salads, two simply marked "Salad"—an Apple Cheese Salad and a Red Apple Cinnamon Salad. Desserts such as the Jell-O poke cake—just called Jell-O Cake—and Glass Pie also appear.[9]

Throughout, the *76* exudes a sense for frugality and advice on how to stretch a meal. The meat-based recipes are the clearest on this point. The recipe for Spanish Rice, for example, calls for any variety of chopped meat, mixed with rice, tomato, and onion. The contributor herself is aware of the recipe's reputation for stretching the budget, noting: "Make Spanish Rice for these affairs when appetites are keen and a little money must feed a lot of hungry folk." Most of the casseroles as well as the recipes in the Meat chapter, indeed, call for ingredients such as chopped meat and stale bread. In the absence of meat (and the second World War's call for meatless meals) many of the casseroles either use canned or processed meat or are vegetarian. In Jessamyn Neuhaus' "Is Meatloaf for Men?" she comments on the image of such recipes, noting that "meatloaf's reputation for thriftiness grew from its ability to incorporate a variety of leftover ground or chopped meat, as well as nonmeat 'stretchers'" (91). This thrift is evident in the sponsors' inclusion of such recipes and accompanying commentary.

Such frugality is also reflected in recipes that do not contain processed ingredients.

There are, for example, several pie recipes, including one called "Vinegar Pie," that seem to consist of little other than brown sugar, butter, and perhaps milk. Such recipes reflect cooks who lived through time periods when few items would have been available to even fill a pie. Ferguson labels these "mock foods," and while *76* does not go to the extreme that he suggests existed—crackers instead of apples, for example, there is a Mock Cherry Pie—made from cranberries—and a Poor Man's Lobster—made from haddock. Most fish in the *76* is also canned or frozen—compared to *Bouquet Garni* where most is fresh.

Class is an important marker in helping readers become closer readers of texts such as cookbooks. Insight into class can help us to more clearly define the texts that we are reading as well as their sponsoring communities. Overall, the class differences in these two cookbooks are very clear, and understanding them contributes to our overall understanding of the self-definitions of the communities.

Conclusion

In her introduction to *Books that Cook*, Marion Nestle notes the many levels on which cookbooks and recipes may be interpreted: "as English tests ripe for close textual analysis, as deeply moving fiction or memoir, as a way to learn about life, as suggestions for what to cook for dinner, or just as a pleasant way to pass time" (xvii). And yet, cookbooks can help us to rhetorically read and participate in community, or as Anne Bower suggests, to create communal identity and to "beautifully [relate] and [shape] a community's time and place and needs and longings and difficulties and delights" (8). This is certainly true with the books that I looked at. In addition to sharing their community history through their recipes, they also reflect material conditions and geographical and traditional identities, filtered and organized by their sponsors. In reading these cookbooks in this way, I am able to create my own definition of what it means to be a literate reader and interpret more about that community from the cookbook itself, to invest it with meaning and create my own narrative. Without a careful reading and literate knowledge of the contents of the cookbooks, I can merely cook and eat.

Endnotes

1. According to Alumnae Association records, there were approximately 20,300 living alumnae in 1978; approximately 500 (2.5%) identified as non-white. Graduation years listed indicate contributions from classes ranging from 1913 to 1980, meaning that contributors ranged in age from 26 to 93 at the time of the 1986 printing.

2. While I was unable to locate census information for Maine, the 1970 census for Newark Valley lists 1,288 residents. While racial information was not broken down by town, in the 1970 census only .9% of the entire county was listed as non-white.

3. This is not always true; as Anne Bower observes in her work on community cookbooks, a tremendous variation in the producers and products is not uncommon. In terms

of the cookbooks, "there are so many of them; most of them aren't accessibly cataloged; and in truth, not all of them are fascinating" (8).

4. They remain so—according to the 2010 Census, Maine's population was 5,377 and Newark Valley's was 3,946—although this makes it nearly a third larger than it was in 1970.

5. The story that I (and a few of my fellow alums) remembered was far more lurid (although likely far less accurate). The rumor was that Deacon Porter's wife had accused him of having an affair with Mary Lyon, the college's founder. Porter had responded with indignation, telling his wife that if this was true, he would eat his hat. Legend had it that she had then steamed it into a pudding and served it to him. I asked approximately 20 alums from a 50 year time span, and most remembered little about the story at all, although all recalled that Deacon Porter's Hat was both served regularly and was not a favorite for eating.

6. Perhaps because of the recipe's existence for at least 150 years, it has leaked beyond the campus walls (it is certainly not because of its appeal as food). A quick Google search reveals an appearance of the recipe in the 1987 *L. L. Bean Book of New New England Cookery*. It is also included in the 1999 *The New England Cookbook: 350 Recipes from Town and Country, Land and Sea*, with the descriptor: "A spiced suet pudding steamed in a tall cylindrical mold. In 1837, at Mount Holyoke College the pudding was named to honor a favorite deacon, and the shape of his stovepipe hat. The dessert is still served at the College on Founder's Day" (521). It seems appropriate that a cookbook meant for women of the college community would have less context surrounding the recipe, and that outside publications would contain more, and yet it seems that the Mount Holyoke women would have perhaps benefitted from the extra information.

7. Of the alums that I surveyed about Deacon Porter's Hat, several told me that they had tried to make the recipe themselves in the intervening years since graduation. One admitted that it was better when she had made it herself, while another confessed that she had found it wholly inedible and had to throw it out. Several made it during weekends where fellow alums were coming to visit.

8. Consumers spent an astonishing 150 million dollars on frozen foods in 1940, for example, but with an increase in the numbers of refrigerators, the products that were being produced, and the number of women in the work force, by 1970 that number had jumped to seven billion dollars (Wallach 139).

9. Jell-O cake generally is comprised of a box mix white cake. Once the cake is cooked, the Jell-O is made and poured over it. Glass Pie is different colors of Jell-O, cut into cubes and combined with whipped cream and served in a pie crust.

Works Cited

76: The Bicentennial Cookbook of The Senior Citizens of Maine and Newark Valley. 1976. Print.
Bouquet Garni. Portland, Connecticut: Waverly Printing Company. 1986. Print.

Bower, Anne. "Bound Together: Recipes, Lives, Stories, and Readings." *Recipes for Reading: Community Cookbooks, Stories, Histories.* Anne L. Bower, Ed. Amherst: U of Massachusetts P, 1997. 1-14. Print.

Brandt, Deborah. "Sponsors of Literacy." *CCC* 49.2 (May 1998): 165-85. Print.

Dojny, Brooke. *The New England Cookbook: 350 Recipes from Town and Country, Land and Sea.* Boston, MA: Harvard Common Press, 1999. Print.

"Eating History." http://eatinghistory.blogspot.com/2006/02/spiedies-of-binghamton-in-new-york-usa.html..12 February 2015. Web.

Eves, Rosalyn Collings. "A Recipe for Remembrance: Memory and Identity in African-American Women's Cookbooks." *Rhetoric Review* 24.3 (2005): 280-97. Print.

Ferguson, Kennan. "Intensifying Taste, Intensifying Identity: Collectivity through Community Cookbooks." *Signs: Journal of Women in Culture and Society* 37.3 (2012): 695-717.

Fleitz, Elizabeth. "Cooking Codes: Cookbook Discourse as Women's Rhetorical Practices." *Present Tense* 1.1 (2010): 1-8. Print.

Heck, Marina de Camargo. "Adapting and Adopting: The Migrating Recipe." *The Recipe Reader: Narratives-Contexts-Traditions.* Janet Floyd and Laurel Forster, Eds. Bodmin, Cornwall, United Kingdom: 2003. 205-218. Print.

Higgins, Lorraine, Elenore Long, and Linda Flower. "Community Literacy: A Rhetoric Model for Personal and Public Inquiry." *Community Literacy Journal* 1.1 (2006): 9-43. Print.

Jones, Judith B. and Evan Jones. *The L.L. Bean Book of New New England Cookery.* New York: Random House, 1987. Print.

Kelly, Alison P. "Choice Receipts from American Housekeepers: A Collection of Digitized Community Cookbooks from the Library of Congress." *The Public Historian.* 34.2 (May 2012): 30-52. Print.

LeBesco, Kathleen. "There's Always Room for Resistance: Jell-O, Gender, and Social Class." Sherrie Inness, Ed. *Cooking Lessons: The Politics of Gender and Food.* Lanham, MD: Rowman and Littlefield, 2001. 129-49. Print.

Leonardi, Susan. "Recipes for Reading: Summer Pasta, Lobster a la Riseholme, and Key Lime Pie." *PMLA* 104.3 (May, 1989) 340-47. Print.

Levi-Strauss, Claude. "The Culinary Triangle." Carole Counihan and Penny VanEsterik, Eds. F*ood and Culture: A Reader.* New York: Routledge, 1997. 28-35.

Lewis, George H. "From Minnesota Fat to Seoul Food: Spam in America and the Pacific Rim." *Journal of Popular Culture.* 34.2 (Fall 2000). 83-105. Print.

Neuhaus, Jessamyn. "Is Meatloaf for Men? Gender and Meatloaf Recipes, 1920-1960." Sherrie Inness, Ed. *Cooking Lessons: The Politics of Gender and Food.* Lanham, MD: Rowman and Littlefield, 2001. 87-109.

Nestle, Marion. Foreward. *Books that Cook: The Making of a Literary Meal.* Cognard-Black, Jennifer and Melissa Goldthwaite, Eds. New York: New York UP, 2014. xv-xviii. Print.

Wallach, Jennifer Jensen. *How America Eats*. Lahnam, MD: Rowman and Littlefield Publishers, 2013. Print.

Warner, France Lester. *On a New England Campus*. New York: Houghton Mifflin, 1937. Web.

Zeigelman, Jane. 97 *Orchard: An Edible History of Five Immigrant Families in One New York Tenement*. New York: Harper, 2010. Print.

Author Bio

Lisa Mastrangelo is an Associate Professor of English and the Director of Composition at Centenary College of New Jersey. Her primary research interests are in nineteenth century writing pedagogy and writing program administration. Her published work has appeared in journals such as *College English*, *Rhetoric Review*, and *College Composition and Communication*.

Feed Your Mind: Cultivating Ecological Community Literacies with Permaculture

Stephanie Wade

> This article proposes *permaculture*, an ecological alternative to industrial agriculture, as a way to design first-year composition and community literacy classes. First, the paper connects permaculture with post-humanism to describe ecological community literacies—the type of knowledge that ecological theorists say we need to navigate the end of the anthropocene. Next, it describes assignments that can lead college students to this knowledge, and finally, it describes actual community literacy projects where college students can lead elementary students through assignments to gain this knowledge.

As a college writing teacher, I often feel that my work—teaching writing at Unity College, a small, private, liberal arts college in Maine devoted to environmentalism—is like the work of farmers making the transition from conventional to organic farming. Just as the farmers face soil depleted of important nutrients, soil that bears the scars of industrial agriculture, soil that is compacted and resistant to change, having been subject to pesticides and chemical fertilizers and misused in the name of profits, I face students depleted of physiological and psychological nutrients, students who bear the scars of conventional education, students who believe their test scores represent their worth and who are resistant to change, having been subject to standardized tests, packaged curricular materials, and rubrics that fail to register creativity, imagination, kindness, and curiosity. The problems I face, like those faced by organic farmers, have been caused, for the most part, by conventional approaches to education and agriculture.

Tracing the histories of conventional agriculture and conventional education reveals that both have been shaped by modernist ideals of progress, by industrialism, and by capitalism in ways that cause harm. Happily, organic farming and other alternatives to conventional agriculture have succeeded in creating ecological farming choices and new food cultures. In this essay, I propose that writing teachers, especially those working on community literacy projects, may find viable alternatives to conventional education by practicing *permaculture*, an ecological alternative to conventional agriculture. I ask that we build on the growing awareness of ecological food choices to promote ecological approaches to education in general and to composition studies in specific, and I demonstrate that community literacy projects are an important feature of ecological approaches to literacy. Lastly, I describe ecological community literacy projects that are grounded in permaculture.

Ecological community literacy projects respond to what Paul Lynch calls the "apocalyptic turn" in composition studies (458). According to Lynch, the apocalyptic turn redefines the work of composition studies today in the context of the end of the anthropocene, the end of the era dominated by human impact on the ecosystems of the planet. Redefining this work requires us to acknowledge our embeddedness in multiple, shifting, dynamic material and ideological worlds, worlds where ideas and lived experience are less stable and less hierarchical that they had appeared in other eras. Several decades ago, postmodern philosophies tried to account for these multiplicities, but they failed to truly attend to the lingering effects of modernism and to adequately account for agency (Jameson; Owens; Gare). Emerging ecological philosophies more fully account for the material effects of our embeddedness in multiple ideological and material worlds (Latour; Morton). This, of course, creates uncertainty, and at the same time it creates hope and room for alternatives. In this paper, I use the term *ecological community literacies* in three ways: first, to describe the type of knowledge Lynch and other ecological theorists say we need to navigate the end of the anthropocene; second, to describe assignments that can lead college students to this knowledge; and third, to describe actual community literacy projects where college students can lead elementary students through assignments to gain greater understanding of themselves in relationship to the multiple communities that comprise their worlds.

Lynch directs us to ideas that are grounded in good research about teaching and learning as well as broader work in ethics, aesthetics, and education, yet such approaches to education conflict with trends in conventional education, such as poor assessment and labor practices that create barriers to projects that require time, space, and funding. Because similar forces have shaped agriculture and education, educators can learn to navigate these forces from farmers and gardeners who use permaculture to design alternatives to conventional farming practices. Below, I provide an overview of permaculture that connects it with ecological approaches to literacy, especially those that are grounded in posthumanism and object-oriented ontology. Then, I review examples of ecological community literacy projects that apply permaculture to education, with the hope that readers will begin to image other types of ecological community literacy projects

I.

Industrial approaches to both agriculture and to education are rooted in the old Cartesian hierarchy that posits humans near God, above the plant and animals and material worlds and that posits human intellect as the supreme human ability. This paradigm, which many call humanism, has reached the end of its usefulness, as we learn from the posthumanists, who explain that the era in which we currently live—dominated by anthropogenic changes such as climate change—is nearing its end and that we need new ideas and practices to the navigate the emerging world. Humanism—the dominant paradigm in the west for the last several hundred years—disseminated important values, such as increasing freedom and dignity for many humans, but these values also wrought destructive changes as they have been used a veil for the values of capital.

Jean Francois Lyotard's 1979 work, *The Postmodern Condition: A Report on Knowledge*, connects changes in education to changes in economics and power. He explains that the humanistic tradition, supported by the emancipation narrative, views education as the route to human freedom, so knowledge in the sciences and humanities gains legitimacy from its liberatory potential. This narrative is threatened in the postmodern world, according to Lyotard, as our disbelief in all master narratives has paved the route for the rise of the performativity narrative and the values of capital, which gain their power from force rather than belief and create problems for agriculture and education because they legitimize knowledge based on efficiency. The performativity narrative serves capital and perpetuates the hierarchies that tie value to economic productivity rather than ecological balance, but vestiges of the emancipation narrative linger, so rhetoric about education associates it with freedom while education practices serve capital.

The effects of the change from the emancipation narrative to the performativity narrative can be seen in the parallels between agriculture and education. In Wendell Berry's history of farming *The Unsettling of America: Culture and Agriculture*, he reports that small family farmers were pushed out as the values of efficiency encouraged the use of technology rather than human and horsepower. On the impact of the business model on farming, Berry writes, "It forces a profound revolution in the farmer's mind: once his investment in land and machines is large enough, he must forsake the values of husbandry and assume those of finance and technology" (45). Ravitch's more recent study of the privatization of K-12 education, *Reign of Error: The Hoax of the Privatization Movement*, similarly assesses the impact of the business model on education. In fact, she explains that the principle of value-added assessment in education came from William Sanders, who first worked on such assessment in agriculture. This model proposes that progress in agriculture and in education be assessed in measurable ways, so we can quantify the value. But, Ravitch points out, many important goals of education cannot be objectively measured and those who support such initiatives do so because they stand to make money from them either through testing contracts, curricular materials, or for-profit charter schools.

In 1974, Bill Molisen and David Holgrem developed a sustainable alternative to industrial agriculture based on ecology. They called it *permaculture*, which stands for permanent agriculture, to emphasize their commitment to soil health, thus laying the groundwork for a system that could be permanent, unlike industrial agriculture, which threatens our food supply by emphasizing profits and convenience at the expense of long-term environmental balance. Bill Molisen explains: "Permaculture is a philosophy of working with, rather than against nature; of protracted & thoughtful observation rather than protracted & thoughtless labour; & of looking at plants & animals in all their functions, rather than treating any area as a single-product system." David Holgrem has recently defined three core values of permaculture: earth care, people care, and fair share. Upon these three values, he has created a list of twelve permaculture design principles. Those that I have used most often in my literary work include: "observe and interact," "produce no waste," and "use and value diversity" ("Permaculture Principles"). I will review how permaculture designers and organic farmers follow these principles, and then I will describe my applications of these principles in my teaching.

Permaculture designers begin by studying the site itself: the soil, water, wind, human, animal, and plant communities that comprise the place, their patterns, habits and needs, following the principle observe and interact. Then, they use this information to assemble an aesthetically, ethically, and ecologically pleasing environment. A permaculture designer may use rain barrels to add a decorative element to a garden, to solve a run off problem, and to provide water. Using one step to create multiple benefits is known as stacking functions. Farmer would have diverse crops and types of livestock on their farms, like Polyface Fram, which Michael Pollan writes about in *The Ominvore's Dilmena*. This diversity shields the farmer from fluctuations in the weather and the economy. Plus, farmers who value diversity by raising crops and livestock produce less waste because resources, like hay, become fuel for cows and then milk and meat for sale as well as manure to enrich the soil for continued growing of crops. In these ways, permaculture attends to the material world, pays serious attention to the elements, and situates humans in relationship to plants, animals, and the elements. By studying permaculture and acting on its principles, then, we can begin to expand our work in the very way that Paul Lynch asks, expanding literacy work so that this work connects participants with multiple communities—human, plant, animal, and elemental.

Bill Molisen explains that permaculture begins with the nose, then the hands, then the back door, and finally, the doorstep. Permaculture is multisensorial embodied work that begins where we are with the material at hand rather than where we hope to go. In this way, it aligns with theories of affect, which creates more room for embodiment and emotional appeals in our discourse and offers a strong theoretical rationale for the value of imaginative writing. Brian Holmes explicitly situates affective and aesthetic discourse in the collapsing systems precipitated by neoliberalism in his book *Escaping the Overcode*. Holmes extends and updates Lyotard's work as he details the master narratives that continue to exert much influence in material and ideological realms, in essence, training people to define themselves as consumers rather than creators, which perpetuates environmental destruction. In order to stop this destruction, Holmes claims we need to engage in affective discourse, which he describes as art that appeals to the senses and reminds us of embodiment. This grounds us in the world of the senses and move us beyond logocentric discourse, but, it is unruly, unpredictable, hard to assess, and not necessarily connected to narrow, financial values, so affective discourse requires us to reframe our work if we aim to move beyond deadly, deadening conventions.

Closer to our field, Rachel Riedner and Kevin Mahoney emphasize the importance of affect in their book *Democracies to Come*. They use the term *rhetorical action* to describe interventions that create alternatives to neoliberalism. The examples they use—post-colonial theory and Zapatista resistance work—include a range of media—

academic writing, political writing, storytelling, and political action—which places their work in the tradition of composition scholars such as Mark Shadle, Robert Davis, Christian Weisser, and Nancy Welch, who urge us to move beyond academic discourse and to engage in what Welch calls "rhetoric from below": the language practices and organized actions employed by marginalized groups to increase their agency.

What I aim to add to this important work is attention to the rhetoric from even further below, from the ground, from the soil that sustains life on earth, where we find important knowledge about the value of diversity, new ideas about identity, and important connections between permaculture and posthumanism—an outgrowth of new materialism that, like permaculture, calls for collaborative rather than hierarchical relationships between humans and other beings, ideas, and objects. Dating back at least as far at Donna Haraway's 1985 "A Manifesto for Cyborgs," new materialist approaches resituate human perception and identity in multiple, shifting contexts in relationship to other people, plants, animals, ideas, and things. Much of Bruno Latour's work on actor network theory rethinks agency as an ongoing collaboration among beings where constraints are opportunities. As I mentioned above, Paul Lynch explains that Latour's work requires composition studies to understand our work in the context of the end of the anthropocene, which connects to the work of posthumanist thinkers, such as Levi Bryant and Tim Morton, who explain that contemporary environmental forces—such as climate change, what Morton calls "a hyperobject" because it is so vast that it evades our apprehension—have toppled the ideological and material hierarchies that supported modernist ideals of humanism.

This has implications for agriculture in that the ideals of convenience and choice, which construct us as consumers, are being replaced with a better understanding of the material constraints wrought by the ecological implications of industrial food production as well as a better understanding of our agency as creators of food via victory gardens, urban vertical farming, participation in community-supported agriculture, and a renewed interested in cooking and preserving food (Katz 2006). This also has implications for education in that it changes our understanding of ourselves and of the type of knowledge we need to navigate an ever-changing world. Next, I explain how ecological community literacies provide such knowledge.

II.

Ecological approaches to literacy date back to Richard Coe's 1975 article "Eco-Logic for the Composition Classroom," which, much like posthumanist theory today, argues for alternatives to analytic-logic, and Marilyn Cooper's 1986 article "An Ecology of Writing," which argues for attention to the contexts of writing to counterbalance the cognitive approaches were favored at that time. In 2001 and 2002, ecological approaches received more sustained and deep attention with the publication of two books: *Composition and Sustainability: Teaching for a Threatened Generation* by Derek Owens and *Natural Discourse: Toward Ecocomposition* by Sidney Dobrin and Christian Weisser. Owens begins with an environmentalist agenda and concludes with ecological theory that proposes reconstructivist design as a means of acknowledging the provisional nature of knowledge and at the same time moving beyond the impasse of postmodernism. In this way, Owens's work aligns with that of theorists who use object-oriented ontology (Morton 2011) and actor-network theory (Latour 2010) to recast our understanding of agency as neither completely free nor completely determined but rather constrained, which also aligns with the work of permaculture designers who ask us to view constraints as possibilities rather than limiting factors. Dobrin and Weisser (2002), coined the term *ecocomposition*, an extension of ecocriticism and ecofeminism, to describe an approach that moves in two directions: to probe rhetorical social constructions of nature and to enable students to exercise their ability to produce discourse, which situates them as predecessors of Paul Lynch and his call for more creative composition and less critique.

Ecological approaches to literacy, mostly called ecocomposition after Dobrin and Weisser's work, share many common features. Reviewing the work of Owens, Dobrin and Weisser, Nedra Reynolds, and M. Syverson as well as four syllabi informed by ecocomposition, I discerned eight important features of ecocomposition: student-centered approaches, place-based assignments, readings with nature themes, interdisciplinarity, public writing, use of new media, service learning, and posthumanism. For the purposes of this article, I will focus on a cluster of features that most closely relate to ecological community literacies- place-based writing, public writing, interdisciplinarity, and community literacy work. First, I will review the research that underpins these features, then I will explain how I employed them, and finally, I will reflect on what my students and I learned.

Place-based writing falls into the tradition of place-based education, an approach to teaching that is used in K-12 settings and beyond, which engages students in work that matters to them by connecting school work with the students' lived experiences and the world outside the classroom (Sobel). Because our lived experiences rarely fall into the seemingly neat academic demarcations of academic disciplines, placed-based writing is inherently interdisciplinary (Davis and Shadle). The interdisciplinary nature of this work is important because the problems that communities face require multiple stakeholders to navigate information from multiple fields. Public writing is both a step towards preparing students to communicate with multiple stakeholders and a response to research that acknowledges the limits of academic discourse, which may be insular (Davis and Shadle; Weisser; Welch). In the tradition of shifting the focus of college writing beyond the campus, community literacy projects take students outside the classroom (Goldblatt).

At Unity College, a school devoted to environmentalism, students enroll in a two-semester sequence of communication classes that integrate writing and speaking. All faculty use place as a theme for these classes, and we lead students through a shared set of formal assignments beginning with a personal place project followed by an informative place project in the first semester and including a public place project and a persuasive place project in the second semester. These classes are informed by ecological approaches to literacy and by permaculture, especially slow observation over time, stacking functions, and valuing diversity.

Students generate material for the personal place project by reading, writing about, and discussing traditional print and multimedia works about place as well as their own experiences. In addition, students draw, talk, and listen to generate material. One activity, inspired by Kristie Fleckenstein's work on spatial literacies, asks students to pick a place that they care about and to sketch an aerial view of that place. Students jot down memories associated with the place on the sticky notes. Next, students present their drawings and memories to each other in small groups of three or four. Students are instructed to think about questions to ask each other while they are listening to their classmates' informal presentations, questions that will help their classmates see where they might include addition material. In this process, students learn about their peers, engage in low stakes peer review, and slowly generate material for formal writing and speaking assignments. This example follows the permaculture principles of engaging in slow observation over time, stacking functions, and valuing diversity. The informal assignments serve multiple purposes: students get multiple, diverse perspectives on their emerging assignments and place; and their topics emerge slowly as they engage in multiple activities using multiple media.

The first formal part of this assignment asks students to either write an essay about the place or to create a multimedia piece about the place. Students have written narratives, created series of vignettes, made PowerPoint slideshows, as well as Prezis and collages about the places that they care about. These multiple media allow students to engage in affective discourse, one route away from logocentrism. For their second formal project, students create a speech about this place. After giving the speech, they continue to revise their first project. We begin with the material at hand, the students' experiences and observations and their connections to places they care about, and students work with this material in a variety of ways. Thus, we continue to follow the permaculture principles of slow observation over time and valuing diversity.

For the next assignment, students return to their drawings. We discuss the circulation of resources (the movement of energy and material through the place) as well as the ecological communities (the human, plant, animal, and other neighbors that inhabit the place or travel through it). Students then sketch in the circulation of resources and the overlapping ecological communities, using sticky notes to down questions that arise as they sketch. This part of the assignment is informed by one devised by Dobrin and Weisser, which has students study the circulation of resources around their collage campus. Our version allows students to select from a variety of places to study. As with the personal project, students share their drawings and sketches and offer each other preliminary feedback to help each other craft good research questions, which we define as questions that are grounded, focused, and interesting.

Students then engage in research with an emphasis on using public information rather than academic research. Underlying the focus on public information are two principles. First, the ability to access and evaluate public information about the places we care about- information about land preservation, trash and recycling, wildlife habitats, planning and development—helps students become informed citizens.

Second, academic research is aimed at specialists, and first semester college students are not yet specialists. Thus, we aim to help students develop a process for writing about new information that is aimed at a general audience rather than specialists. In this way, we encourage interdisciplinary work and we encourage students to engage in public discourse, two features of ecological approaches to literacy. We continue to follow the permaculture principles of working with the material at hand, in this case by selecting public genres that are accessible to students. We also employ this principle by having students create question rooted in their observations that take them beyond their immediate experience and that connect them with ecological communities.

In the second semester, students may return to the questions from the first semester and expand them or devise new questions. They use these questions to engage in library research and to develop two major products- a persuasive research appear and a public document. We follow the principle of slow observation over time in that students may continue to study one topic over the course of two semesters and to learn more about this topic through different types of research, through drafting and feedback and revising, and through translating their material into multiple genres. In pushing students to use multiple types of research and multiple genres, we follow the permaculture principle of cultivating diversity and the imperative to produce no waste. The students' work—their research questions and other material—serves as the compost for the next projects in the series. For the public document, they select an audience outside the class and select a genre that would be appropriate for their chosen audience. They then use their research to compose a document for this audience. Finally, they distribute the document to the audience and write about their experiences. The practice of distributing public documents connects students with communities outside the classroom and allows students to teach outside communities about ecological community literacies.

For example, one student wrote about a family camp for his personal place project. For his informative project, he began with a question based on his own experience and observations. As a duck hunter, he had noticed fewer and fewer ducks over the years, so, for the informative project, he researched duck migration patterns in northern Maine and found that they had indeed been declining. The next semester, he continued to research duck migration patterns and found links between this and climate change. For the public project, he created a pamphlet aimed at hunters to teach them about climate change. He distributed the pamphlet at Cabala's, a store that sells hunting and other outdoor gear. He reported that his audience was responsive to his research.

Another student more directly addressed the value of ecological community literacies and the impact of permaculture pedagogies on her learning. She began with memories of walking the trails behind her home in Connecticut. Her research took her to an exploration of the environmental impact of a water park in a former quarry near her home. In the second semester, she continued to research the ecology of the Connecticut River Valley, she wrote a paper that advocated for more ecological approaches to recreation, and she created a blog aimed at her home community to teach them about the Connecticut River Valley. As she wrote on her blog:

> ... recently ... I took on the project of developing an understanding of the ecology of the Connecticut River...I realized that the best way to care for our natural homes, is to try to understand them, so that decisions about human living are made with these places in mind. Through this page, I hope to share a greater understanding of the Connecticut River, which is home to me, as well as all of the people living in Connecticut Riverside towns, not to mention the biodiversity of insects, plants, fish, birds, mammals and other organisms that find their ecological niche in the river.

Thus, the student explicitly identifies the value of ecological community literacies and defines her work as sharing such knowledge with her community. Later in the semester, she described the impact of the course on her own understanding of herself:

> Before taking Composition and Communication, I felt bitter about the experiences I had with writing and speaking in high school—like I was at a dead end ... However, by using the recursive process in class, and utilizing different methods of generating material, I found that I actually contained a fountain of ideas.

Here, the student explains the deadening impact of her high school experiences and how the permaculture approach allowed her to connect with ideas in herself.

These ecological community literacy projects ask students to attend to multiple communities and relationships. In addition, as students share their work with each other, they learn about the ways in which their communities are unique and in which they are similar. For example, one semester in one of my classes, three students wrote about growing up on the east coast along the shore. Each noticed changes in the lobster industry. From each other, they learned that the problems facing their communities were part of larger trends.

The community literacy class I taught in 2012—one option by which Unity College students could satisfy their community-based learning requirement—also followed permaculture principles and promoted ecological communities, so it serves as another example of stacking functions. Students began by reading and writing literacy narratives. Next, these students created personal place projects much like those described above, but these students were required to also create a visual artifact about the places they selected. Over several weeks in the middle of the semester, the college students traveled to a nearby elementary school and worked with a mixed class of fourth and fifth graders. Students worked in groups comprised of two college students and two or three elementary students. During our first visit to the school, we worked on the place-based drawing to generate material. During our second visit, we worked on informal peer review and drafting. During our third visit, we worked on revising. For our fourth and final visit, we brought trifold boards and helped the students assemble displays. The next week, the elementary school students traveled to our college campus and displayed their work along with the work of the college students. In attendance was a class of fourth graders from a neighboring district.

Like the place-based assignment sequence, the writing projects created in this class helped students cultivate ecological community literacies in a number of ways. The college students learned more about the local communities that comprise Waldo County by working with school children, who shared stories about growing up in places, some of which were marked by severe rural poverty. The fourth and fifth grade students learned more about their human, plant, and animal neighbors by composing and sharing their projects. In addition, students from separate parts of Waldo County learned more about each other and about the ecological communities that comprise the county.

I will teach another community literacy class in the fall of 2015. The college students in this class will have already completed the two-semester, place-based writing sequence I described above, so they will be able to expand upon this work and drawn upon it as we develop workshops for local school children. This assignment sequences follows the permaculture principles described above. In addition, I aim to use ecopoetic aesthetics to deepen my students understanding of the importance of affective discourse.

If this creative writing class is successful and students want to continue working on the community literacy project, I hope to have the ability to run a class solely focused on community literacy in the spring of 2016. This class would also allow college students to work towards their graduation requirements, as it would fulfill their community based learning requirement, which aligns with the principle of permaculture that advocates stacking functions- solutions that address multiple problems and offer multiple benefits, such as the use of rain barrels to prevent erosion from water run-off that also creates a renewable water source. If this works, I will have a structure in place for students to begin to explore community literacy in their first-year general education classes, to deepen this exploration in a creative writing class each fall, and to expand it via a community literacy class the following spring. This would allow me to maintain an ongoing relationship with the local schools and to bring in colleagues from other disciplines to develop ongoing, place-based research projects where our students would work with students in local k-12 schools to improve literacy in terms of communication and in terms of understanding of the human, plant, animal, and material worlds.

What posthumanism adds to community literacy is our responsibility to include our plant, animal, and material neighbors in our definition of community. This means listening to the material world and understanding the material world as capable of producing knowledge. Permaculture provides us with design principles to put posthumanist philosophy into practices: slow observation over time, working with energy flows, paying attention to the margins, and promoting diversity rather than monoculture. Permaculture and posthumanism allow us to cultivate what Marilyn Cooper calls "a pedagogy of responsibility" (quoted in Lynch 459). They allow us to answer Brian Holmes's question "How do you rearrange the stars above your head to open up unexpected ground beneath your feet?" by teaching us that we are the stars and we are the ground, the boundaries between head and feet and stars and ground are temporary, and we are all the same matter and all matter the same.

Works Cited

Bryant, Levi. "Thoughts on Posthumanism." *Larval Subjects*. 10 Nov 12. Web. 18 Mar 15.
Coe, Richard. "Eco-Logic for the Composition Classrooom." *CCC* 26.3 (1975): 232-237. Web. 05 May 15.
Cooper, Marilyn. "The Ecology of Writing/" *College English* 48 (1986): 364-75. Web. 05 May 15.
Cushman, Ellen. "Sustainable Service Learning Programs." *CCC* 54.1 (Sept 2002): 40-65. Web. 05 May 15.
Davis, Robert and Mark Shadle. *Teaching Multiwriting: Reasearching and Composing with Multiple Genres, Media, Disciplines, Cultures*. Carbondale: Southern Illinois University Press, 2007. Print.
Dobrin, Sidney I. and Christian Weisser. *Natural Discourse*. Albany: SUNY Press, 2002. Print.
Berry, Wendell. *The Unsettling of America: Culture and Agriculture*. 3rd ed. San Francisco: Sierra Club Books, 1996. Print.
Hemenway, Toby. Gaia's Garden: *A Guide to Home-Scall Permaculture*. 2nd ed. White River Junction: Chelsea Green, 2009. Print.
Fleckstein, Kristie. *Embodied Literacies: Imageword and a Poetics of Teaching*. Carbondale: Southern Illinois UP, 2003. Print.
Gare, Arran. "Narratives and the Ethics and Politics of Environmentalism: The Transformative Power of Stories." *Theory and Science*. 2001. Web. 01 Sept 14.
Goldblatt, Eli. *Because We Live Here: Sponsoring Literacy Writing Beyond the College Curriculum*. Cresskill, NJ: Hampton Press, 2007. Print.
Haraway, Donna. "A Cyborg Manifesto: Science, Technology, and Socialist Feminism in the Late Twentieth Century." European Graduate School. 1991. Web. 15 Mar 15.
Holgrem, David. "Permaculture Design Principles." "Permaculture Principles. Web. 10 April 15.
Holmes, Brian. "Escape the Overcode: Activist Art in the Control Society." *Continential Drift: The other side of neoliberal globalisation*. Web. 05 Mar 15.
Katz, Sandor Ellix. *The Revolution Will Not Be Microwaved: Inside America's Underground Food Movement*. Great River Junction: Chelsea Green, 2006.
Latour, Bruno. "Reassembling the Social: An Introduction to Actor-Network-Theory." *Clarendon Lectures in Management Studies*. 2005. Web. 12 May 15.
Lawton, Jennifer. "About." On the Connecticut River. 23 Apr 13. Web. 15 Jul 15.
Lynch, Paul. "Composition's New Thing: Bruno Latour and the Apocalyptic Turn in Composition Studies." *College English* 7.5 (2011): 458-467. Web 07 May 13.

Lyotard, Jean-Francios. *The Postmodern Condition: A Report on Knowledge*. Trans. Geoff Bennington and Brian and Massumi. Minneapolis: University of Minnesota Press, 1979. Print.

Molisen, Bill. "Permaculture: Design for Living." Context Institute. 1991. Web. 28 Mar 15.

_____, *About Permaculture*. Web. 25 Mar 2015.

Morton, Timothy. "Here Comes Everything: The Promise of Object-Oriented Ontology." *Qui Parle* 19 (2):163-190. 2011. Web. 07 Jan 15.

_____. *Hyperobjects: Philosophy and Ecology at the End of the World*. Minneapolis: University of Minnesota Press, 2013. Print.

Owens, Derek. *Composition and Sustainability Teaching for a Threatened Generation*. Urbana, Illinois: NCTE, 2001. Print.

Pollan, Michael. *The Ominvore's Dilemma: A Natural History of Four Meals*. New York: Penguin Books, 2006. Print.

Ravitch, Diane. *Reign of Error: The Hoax of the Privatization Movement and the Danger to America's Public Schools*. NY: Vintage, 2014.

Riedner, Rachel and Kevin Mahoney. *Democracies to Come: Rhetorical Action, Neoliberalism, and Communities of Resistence*. Lexington Books, 2008. Print.

Reynolds, Nedra. *Geographies of Writing: Inhabiting Places and Encountering Difference*. Carbondale: Southern Illinois University Press, 2002. Print

Sobel, David. "Place-Based Education: Connecting Classrooms and Community." *Antiochen.Edu*. Web. 23 May 15.

Syverson, M, *The Wealth of Reality*. Carbondale: Southern Illinois University Press, 1999. Print.

Weisser, Christian. *Moving Beyond Academic Discourse: Composition Studies and the Public Sphere*. Carbondale: Southern Illinois University Press, 2002. Print.

Welch, Nancy. *Living Room: Teaching Public Writing in a Privitized World*. Portsmouth: Heinmann, 2006. Print.

Author Bio

Stephanie Wade is an Associate Professor of Writing and the Director of Writing at Unity College, a college devoted to environmentalism in Unity, Maine.

Book & New Media Reviews

Saul Hernandez, Intern
Georgia College and State University

Ryan Cresawn, Intern
University of Arizona

From the Book & New Media Review Editor's Desk
Jessica Shumake
University of Arizona

In a recent meeting with middle and high school teachers in a rural mining town twelve blocks from the Mexican border, as part of a National Writing Project grant focusing on argumentative writing, I experienced the power of in-person collaboration as I took notes on teachers' classroom-tested approaches for teaching argumentation. In my current university appointment I design curricula for fully online courses, which requires constant technological innovation and little face-to-face interaction. The practical strategies the Douglas Unified School District teachers shared not only resonated with many of the classroom practices I remembered from face-to-face teaching, but also humbled me because of their generosity and willingness to share their very best ideas. The same can be said of the keyword authors and reviewers featured in this issue.

This issue's keyword essay, with its emphasis on social movement and change, sets the stage for the reviews that follow it. If social movements are concerned with the maintenance and alteration of symbolic and material reality, then it follows that self-initiated rhetorical acts—in this case, selfies—can be as much a declaration of a shared sense of revolutionary energy as an expression of solipsistic self-regard. Melanie Carter and Amanda Fields' semester-long partnership to teach research writing and rhetorical analysis, with students in Cairo and Tucson, had numerous outcomes. Carter and Fields' reflection on their collaboration takes risks and puts forward that perhaps they co-opted a genre that students would otherwise engage in without teachers monitoring them. Then again, Carter and Fields argue, the genre of the selfie is capacious and protean enough to contribute to students' sense of themselves as rhetorical critics and global citizens. Students' desires to create rhetorically impactful selfies enabled their engagement with one another and also constrained discussions of their differing investments in the genre due to the way selfies impacted public discourse during Arab Spring. Ultimately, Egyptian and American students affirmed their visions for the kinds of change they desired to see in the world based, in part, on their lived experience and communal values. As Carter and Fields suggest, the word 'selfie' mislabels as much as it labels their students' productive back and forth dialogue about the use of social media for activist ends.

Brad Jacobson's review of Todd Ruecker's *Transiciones: Pathways of Latinas and Latinos Writing in High School and College* describes the writing transitions in the lives of Latina/o students and calls for thinking beyond the dualities of home culture and school culture. Given that what happens beyond the walls of the university "matters much more" in terms of supporting the literacy transitions, retention, and graduation rates of Latina/o students, those working in writing program administration and writing instruction are called upon to "work for much broader and ambitious transformations" both beyond and within their institutions. Jacobson agrees with Ruecker's assessment that "institutions can and must change." Furthermore, Jacobson reflectively observes that there is "no silver bullet" to support struggling students or to aid them to resist dominant cultural assumptions that underestimate what they can accomplish. Nonetheless, community engagement researchers must attend to how to implement sustainable pedagogical practices that anticipate the "unpredictable nature of students' paths to and through college."

Jessica Pauszek's engaging review of Erica Abrams Locklear's *Negotiating a Perilous Empowerment: Appalachian Women's Literacies* powerfully illustrates how acquiring writing and communication skills is double-edged, ambiguous, and contradictory. Daniel Bernal's take on Amy Wan's *Producing Good Citizens: Literacy Training in Anxious Times* reminds us that overplaying "literacy and higher education as the preferred road to citizenship" can erase the multifaceted social, cultural, political, and economic hurdles immigrants face as they seek to gain life opportunities. The final review, Erika Dyk's discussion of Hazel Carter's *Creating Effective Community Partnerships for School Improvement*, recommends openness as a framework for practitioners and theorists of community literacy who are invested in school reform and school-community collaboration.

Selfie

Amanda Fields
Fort Hays State University

Melanie Carter
The American University in Cairo

Keyword Essay

As more and more multimodal projects emerge through writing program curricula, and as community literacy projects redefine what it means to facilitate change and reciprocity through generating multiple texts for multiple audiences, we think it would be useful to consider the significance and prevalence of the selfie as a genre, particularly in regard to its potential power to inspire social activism and critical consciousness.

In 2013, *Time* magazine published the cover story "The Selfiest Cities in the World," which reported on a geotagging project of the top 100 places where selfies had appeared on Instagram, including, at the head of the list, Makati (Philippines), Manhattan (New York), Miami (Florida), Anaheim and Santa Ana (California), and Petaling Jaya (Wilson). While *Time* magazine's methods were flawed (e.g., not all selfies are tagged as such, nor do all appear on Instagram), the prevalence of selfies across several regions and cultures is clear. Further, while the selfie as a genre is not confined to a specific age group, digital trends are often assumed to be the realm of youth, and, therefore, selfies are often linked in popular media with assumptions about youth, e.g., that technology such as the smartphone has disconnected them from healthy interpersonal relations. In 2013, *Time* also focused on "The Me Me Me Generation." The May 20, 2013 cover depicts a young woman lying on her stomach, legs up, staring into her smartphone, which she is holding in a position that suggests she is taking a selfie. This issue offers a discussion about why millennials suffer from entitlement issues and how they "will save us all" (Stein).

This emphasis on young people—their potentiality as well as the ways they may disappoint—is not new, of course. Young people are often divided into those who must develop into productive citizens and those who are deviant and must be contained. Susan Talburt and Nancy Lesko note that adolescence is a term that allows for certain kinds of narratives to exist. Since the 1880s, and with the emergence of the concept of adolescence from G. Stanley Hall, youth have been trained to be disciplined citizens, or "potential offender[s]," or members of subcultures. Such categories contribute to the idea that youth are always "'becoming,' … their bodies, actions, and emotions … read as evidence of their immaturity" (Talburt and Lesko 14). Henry Giroux's sobering assessment is that youth are no longer viewed as a "social investment" but either as "consumers" or "troubling, reckless, dangerous persons" (3). Because of the entrenched nature of youth categories, Lesko and Talburt call those who work with youth to be wary of interventions and "new" approaches to this work, asking how these activities "recirculate discourses that universalize youth categorically" (19).

Talburt and Lesko's discussion of the ways that youth are categorized helps clarify the context influencing the 2013 cover of *Time*, where we see a depiction of a teenager, comfortable in her own privilege. She is focused on herself and the way she presents to the world, yet she seems to lack concern for that world around her, preferring the screen she stares into. Assumptions about class, race, gender, and nationality are evident. Here is the white American teenager, taking a selfie. She is entitled but carries some abstract adult hope of preserving and transforming society for the better. It is a progress narrative with obvious limitations. The popular media lens tends to convey the selfie as emblematic of the shallowness and privilege of (often white) contemporary youth, and the genre is understood from this limited perspective. We are interested in shifting this narrative about youth and in rethinking the genre of selfie (and genres similar to the selfie) as a medium for collaboration and social transformation.

In this essay we discuss the emergence of the term "selfie" in popular media and its status as indicative of navel-gazing digital transference. Next, we suggest that the genre of the selfie is flexing to accommodate social movement, and we consider the rhetorical significance of the declarative impulses accompanying selfies. We then discuss a literacy partnership between composition students in the United States and in Egypt, during which we experimented with a selfie assignment that served as an introduction between classes as well as a way for students to reveal social issues they found most urgent to their lives. Our project has caused us to reflect on how the genre of the selfie is forming, has formed, and is already transforming in ways that show potential for social movement and critical thinking. We believe that the selfie as a genre is well worth pedagogical exploration and that such an exploration could inform community literacy studies.

A Brief History of the Selfie

At this point, selfies as we know them today seem to be more than a passing fad, so much so that "selfie" was the Oxford Dictionaries' 2013 Word of the Year. The earliest usage of "selfie" reported by Oxford Dictionaries was in 2002 via an Australian internet forum: "*Um, drunk at a mates 21st, I tripped ofer [sic] and landed lip first (with front teeth coming a very close second) on a set of steps. ... I had a hole about 1cm long right through my bottom lip. And sorry about the focus, it was a selfie*" (qtd. in Pearlman). From the start, it seems the selfie has been associated with deviant behavior. And yet that original use was actually part of a chat forum request for advice: the writer, posting under the topic "Dissolvable stitches" wondered "whether licking his lips would make his stitches dissolve too soon" (qtd. in Pearlman).

The earliest, still searchable, instance of an internet definition of "selfie" appears to have been on Urban Dictionary in 2005. Defined by "wa143aaaaah," a "selfy" is a "self portrait of yourself usually by teen girls." It isn't until 2012 that "selfie" is again defined on the site, and it is still associated with "girls," this time specified as "girls aged 12–21" (Bobwilllong). A further definition includes "a person taking a picture of themselves at arm's length" (Tra_lalaaa).

Selfies are often discussed as harmful, perhaps even toxic, for human relationships and self-esteem because they reflect an unhealthy absorption with self-image. Selfies call up sassy side stares, "duck faces," the presentation of the body for the assumed gaze. Social media profiles are critiqued for showing only the "best" side of a person, or an ironic worst side. They are not, critics would argue, the real self; rather, an ideal self is displayed for others to gaze at, gawk at, and make comparisons with.

The medium of selfies—snapped and shared electronically and thus, often, publicly, has raised concerns about the effects of such sharing and image presentation on youth. A May 2013 Pew Research study of teen and adult social networks and Twitter revealed that 91% of teens posted photos of themselves on social media, up from 79% in 2006 (Pew). Young women were also more likely to post photos of themselves (Pew), leading to concerns about their "high risk for internalization of negative ideals that lead to self-objectification, dissociation, and/or self-harm" (Nguyen 3). Again, these concerns seem to stem from a specific emphasis on whether youth will be harmed, rather than in how selfies could be not only a significant (not always negative) part of identity development or even a useful genre for social consciousness.

Selfie Collaboration

One thing we can take from *Time's* "selfiest" cities is that this is a worldwide phenomenon with potentially different meanings across cultures. We explored this possibility in a recent collaboration between writing classes at The University of Arizona and The American University in Cairo. As instructors with teaching experience both in the U.S. and abroad, and as former colleagues at The American University in Cairo, we were interested in ways we could create a cross–cultural literacy partnership that challenged students to think deeply about their relationships to language and action. Specifically, our joint theme was related to revolution, resistance, and creativity. One of our goals was to help students acknowledge the various ways resistance might manifest—where communicative efforts might be more or less effective and why. For Egyptian students particularly, it was an effort to help them see beyond a definition of revolution that for most of them was shaped exclusively by the events of January 2011.

We were inspired to design a selfie assignment after reading about the Lebanese #notamartyr protest of 2013. The campaign had been initiated when 16-year-old Mohammed Chaar, a bystander, was killed during the assassination via bombing of former Minister of Finance Mohamad Chatah (Sonne). Outrage over the country's continued violence—and over media coverage that focused primarily on the death of a politician rather than Mohammad Chaar—resulted in thousands of sympathizers posting selfies on Facebook and Twitter with protest messages on placards and paper, each message including the hashtag #notamartyr. The selfie messages often featured a stern, saddened person with a statement about the effects of the violence in Lebanon.

Most selfies were a declaration. For instance, one sign read: "I don't want to have to guess which neighbourhood my loved one will be murdered in. I don't want to have to say this is normal. #notamartyr" (Nashrullah).

Inspired by the #notamartyr campaign, we designed a selfie assignment that asks students to post about an issue they care about. Our purpose was to connect students' working definitions of revolution and resistance to issues they already felt were important, and to allow students, by appearing with their statements, ownership of their ideas in a way they might not feel with conventional academic writing. The assignment is intended to be a useful introduction to the concepts of creativity, resistance, and revolution. In addition, the assignment is meant to prompt questions about the effects or possibilities of on-the-ground revolution and resistance spawned through new media communications. This supported the purpose of exploring multimodal writing as potentially key components of revolution and resistance.

After reading about and discussing the #notamartyr protest and coming up with initial working definitions of revolution, students added a "selfie" photo to a Google Docs shared with both classes. This photo was accompanied by a declaration or comment about the issue along with a hashtag that stated "myrevolution" or a variation, such as #myrevolutionaryact. After analyzing the presentation of the #notamartyr samples we had viewed, we asked students to reflect upon their rhetorical choices as they composed their selfies. Consider all aspects of the composition and message, we said, and construct the photograph while understanding that the entire composition will be analyzed as a statement: Your peers will consider not only the protest message, but decisions about typeface, clothing, color choices, composition and then respond with comments and questions. The selfie will introduce you, or some part of you, to your colleagues. What do you want to show about yourself? What do you wish not to reveal? In constructing the assignment, we knew that some students would choose not to include their faces or any part of their bodies in the selfies, and we wanted them to think about the opportunities and rhetorical effects of such choices.

We opted to have students present on a Google Docs rather than Twitter or Tumblr. It was the easiest way to invite a large group to participate and edit, particularly when all students held university email accounts through Gmail. While we could have made the experience more public by going on Twitter proper and asking students to tweet with this hashtag, this would have required all students to have a Twitter account and to be ready for potential public ramifications. While much of our curriculum asks students to think about the implications of public arguments, the selfie assignment was meant to be understood as a safe (as possible) space. Google Docs, as a medium, creates the potential for mistakes (e.g., students accidentally pasting their selfies over others, losing comments, etc.). The document had the potential to be messy, as revolutions so often are. A Google Doc is also a living document. The document, too, lends itself to the ways in which collaborative texts and discussions can be useful for social movement, as well as how conflict (in relation to beliefs about what is or isn't important in relation to social change) might be addressed. Additionally, the assignment counted for a small portion of the course grade, so students were encouraged to experiment and not to worry about repercussions as long as they were being thoughtful in explaining their choices and participating in good faith.

There are several intersections of class and privilege at AUC, a private liberal arts college in a country with a small elite, that are not as clear at a public research institution in Arizona. Through the selfie assignment, these differences emerged both subtly and in a more direct way, through the composition of the selfie photographs as well as the protest messages students chose. Many of the selfies were typical: e.g., educational expense as a burden, a "debt sentence." However, when a group of students from Arizona decided to explore educational debt further and wanted to design a survey about educational debt for Egyptian students, they soon discovered the cultural differences, where, in Egypt, public institutions are free (creating an entirely different set of problems) and the system for student loans is much different and less extensive than in the U.S. Other common selfie themes include the desire to express oneself (e.g., tattoos) and commitment to a specific issue (e.g., food production). Several of the selfies stood out, eliciting powerful and often sympathetic commentary from students in the peer class.

One of the first to be uploaded was by an Arizona student with a visible genetic condition. In his selfie, he looks straight into the camera, with his message, "I dream of a world where NO ONE has to live like me," and #medicalrevolution and #supportstemcellresearch in black marker on white paper directly underneath his face. This selfie received the most comments between the classes. Egyptian students, in their responses, drew parallels between the strength of his act in posting the selfie and the powerful acts they had witnessed from citizens during the 2011 revolution. One Egyptian student wrote: "I think this picture is the most successful because I felt like it was speaking to me and urging me to do something even though I am not really affected by it or suffering from it. And this is how a revolutionary act should be so that in the end a true revolution can be formed." Another Egyptian student wrote: "I love your courage, simplicity, and the way you figure out yourself. ... Your choice of the sentence, words and representing yourself with your message made the selfie a masterpiece. ... Many people have written books and gave speeches to deliver your meaningful message which you was able to do it through one selfie, which is something amazing."

While many of the students imitated the setup of the #notamartyr selfies, we noticed some distinctions between the American and Egyptian students' choices. For instance, several of the Egyptian students used drawings to convey their message rather than a photo of themselves. Egyptian students more frequently identified issues in abstract terms, such as the desire for "peace." One selfie, uploaded by an AUC student, shows a piece of paper with a handwritten message: "Reconcile before conflicts burn us to ashes." The message is accompanied by a hand-drawn map of the world, and the student gazes into the camera, the piece of paper covering everything below his eyes, the right side of the paper in flames. "The use of burning the paper he is holding places emphasis on the urgency of the issue," one student responded. " ... he has little time to hold the paper before the fire reaches him." While we do not want to draw broad conclusions here, and this is not the purpose of our essay, we did find it of interest that the students who had been present for a major uprising tended toward more abstract messages than the American students, who were mainly interested in showing their ties to one specific social issue.

If we had this assignment to do over again, we would think more about the effects of coherence in relation to the scaffolding of the rest of the course, in which students were asked to collaborate with others on multimodal projects centered on ideas about revolution and resistance. A major difference between our project and the Lebanese campaign was a lack of coherence in terms of belonging to a particular situation. Both groups of students responded with protest messages that were individual. It was clear through student response to the selfies, though, that students were interested in discovering similarities. This sense of expectation, of how students might have been able to speak from group to group because of the shared experiences outside of their individual protests, ultimately had a subtle distancing effect.

It was clear during class discussion that Egyptian students felt unified, even in their individual protests. The majority of the selfies did not reference the 2011 revolution, and yet the students had their particular political situation firmly in mind, no matter what they were protesting in their individual selfies. It was as if the political context, the experience of the revolution, had added a depth, a dimension, that they clearly felt was layered over or under their own private messages. In the case of the American students, issues were often either extremely personalized, as with the student who photographed the tattoos on her back as a way of protesting discrimination toward those who have tattoos, or issues were iterations of national news stories, such as the statement that education is a "debt sentence." The American students did not seem to convey a shared sense of community around their beliefs and experiences in the way expressed by Egyptian students.

Selfies can take up—and might attempt to dismantle—a variety of social hierarchies. Our students' collaboration was no different, since the selfie assignment provided a forum for their image presentation as well as a way to document an aspect of personality not always seen in a snapshot, perhaps especially when that snapshot is carefully composed. As deliberate acts of resistance, and as unconventional assignments completed as part of traditional coursework, the selfies also address the political and academic hierarchies that value standards and stability, and place stability in a valued position, whereas transition or "development" or even creativity, may often be placed on a lower, shakier rung. This recognized hierarchy, which students often struggle to attend to, became a particularly interesting structure held against AUC students' own belief that their country's (and sometimes their own) experience elevated them *above* their U.S. peers, with one student commenting after our selfie posts that the AUC class had less to gain from collaborative interaction since Arizona students had not experienced a full-scale political revolution and were concerned instead with "low-stakes," more personal, issues such as body image, animal rights, or efforts to shift thinking about immigration.

Whether Egyptian students believed the collaboration selfies were "revolutionary" or not, all of them saw creative potential in the composed images. The images also had a clear rhetorical impact, an important point in a research writing class. A reflection assignment at the end of the term asked them to consider both types of messages, and ultimately, decide whether a research essay *could* also be creative. Several responded with a strong "No." Research writing, they said, and in fact all academic writing, was by definition structured, boring, hemmed in by rules. This was what made the selfie assignment so invigorating for them. It allowed an avenue for expression that was brief and powerful and in which they felt they had a voice. The majority who felt that research essays could be creative tended to focus on a research essay's ability to express a creative idea. The answer to the research question could—even should—be creative. It should express a perspective not yet discussed. But none addressed the possibility of creative composition: for the composing process to be creative, or for the conventional essay structure to be altered.

It is easy to dismiss selfies as narcissistic and shallow. And many, seemingly, are. But every genre has its opportunities to flex, extend, and inhabit new territory. Selfies are always statements: that we are here. That we are both apart from and a part of a community. Perhaps they state that we stand for something. They allow our acts and our accidents (those ill-chosen selfie moments) to be acknowledged and even scrutinized. "Selfie" is a common term by now, but its association with youth has not yet faded, just as our mythologies about youth—that they are always becoming, that they go through developmental stages with parameters that are easily defined, that they are "they" and not "us"—are difficult to shake. We wonder, then, to what extent the selfie as a genre might be associated with social movement or change, and to what extent young people might perceive selfies in such a way.

We come away from our collaborative selfie assignment, and the concept of the selfie, understanding the richness with which selfies might be explored for community literacy purposes. There is much work that can be done. Beyond a brief and helpful article in 2014 in *College Teaching* called "The Selfie as a Pedagogical Tool in a College Classroom," selfies are not discussed much in literacy and writing studies. Stacey Margarita Johnson, et al., argue that their "students are building community through the production and distribution of the digital self-portrait" (119) and detail three pedagogical techniques making use of the selfie: the ice-breaker, a translation exercise, and an experiential-learning activity. They argue that selfie assignments "meet students where they are" and demonstrate how social media can be used "for more meaningful purposes" (120). This is a useful start to reflecting upon the possibilities of selfies, and we would add that constructing a thoughtful analysis of the selfie presentation is part of our main concern, as students are often (but not always, we realize) leaps and bounds ahead of adults in social media usage and savvy. But we want to take care not to overuse spaces where young people may have previously felt safe or unwatched by adults.

We believe that future pedagogical work might focus on the ways in which selfies can share many characteristics with other genres that speak up for change and call for coalition. A selfie is a reflection, for instance, but how might the genre of the selfie allow for messages to be performed and received in ways that account for the fluidity of our identifications? In this case, Adela C. Licona's *Zines in Third Space: Radical Cooperation and Borderlands Rhetorics*, offers the concept of "reverso" as a way to understand how third space subjects might respond to normative narratives not through counternarrative but, rather, through refraction, which conjures up a more innovative and complicated way of perceiving (24). Such work can challenge us in the composition of texts about ourselves and the issues we care the most about to ask creative questions and go beyond a direct message. At the same time, we think of Karma R. Chávez's work in Queer Migration Politics: Activist Rhetoric and Coalitional Possibilities, in which Chávez examines the use of manifestos in Tucson community organizations Coalición de Derechos Humanos and Wingspan. A selfie is often a declaration, and an implied manifesto. But a selfie, along with other statements about who one is, individually or in connection with a group, can also be a space for the development of critical consciousness. Chávez connects the coalitional work of manifestos to Aimee Carrillo Rowe's concept of differential belonging: "Continuing to value impurity and multiplicity, one does not have to 'be' a certain identity in order to do political work. Who someone is, is constructed by where they already belong, and where they choose to belong." Such an understanding can lead to "coalitional subjectivities" that allow for people to perceive conflicts that are usually separated (27).

Manifestos, as Chávez writes, "are not dialogic texts" (48); nor, one might assume, are selfies. Yet selfies, like the manifestos Chávez describes, are capable of flexing as a genre. We declare who we are to connect and divide simultaneously. Within those declarations are the unpinnable identifications that move us to common cause and conflict in spaces we do not always expect. We would call upon ourselves in our next sojourn into the selfie assignment to think more deeply about the possibilities for coalition and conflict that our students, and those who participate in other community literacy spaces, offer.

Works Cited

Bobwilllong. "Selfies." *Urban Dictionary*. N.p., 15 Jul. 2012. Web. 14 Dec. 2014.

Chávez, Karma R. *Queer Migration Politics: Activist Rhetoric and Coalitional Possibilities*. Urbana: University of IL Press, 2013. Print.

Giroux, Henry A. *Youth in a Suspect Society: Democracy or Disposability?* London: Palgrave Macmillan, 2010. Print.

Johnson, Stacey M., Stephen Maiullo, et al. "The Selfie as a Pedagogical Tool in a College Classroom." *College Teaching* 62.4 (2014): 119–120. Print.

Licona, Adela C. *Zines in Third Space: Radical Cooperation and Borderlands Rhetoric*. Albany, NY: State U of New York, 2012. Print.

Nashrulla, Tasneem. "41 Powerful Messages From A Selfie Protest In Lebanon." *BuzzFeed*. N.p., 7 Jan. 2014. Web. 12 Dec. 2014.

Nguyen, Amy J. "Exploring the Selfie Phenomenon : The Idea of Self-preservation and Its Implications among Young Women." Thesis. Smith College, 2014. *Exploring the Selfie Phenomenon: The Idea of Self-preservation and Its Implications among Young Women*. Web. 15 Dec. 2014.

Pearlman, Jonathan. "Australian Man 'invented the Selfie after Drunken Night Out.'" *The Telegraph*. Telegraph Media Group, 19 Nov. 2013. Web. 25 Oct. 2014.

Pew Research Internet Project. *Sharing, connections, and privacy in the world of teen social media*. (Data file). Washington, DC: Pew Research Center, 2013. Web. 15 Oct. 2014.

Sonne, Kirstin. "#NotAMartyr: Lebanon's Protest Selfies." *Nouse*. N.p., 4 Feb. 2014. Web. 25 Oct. 2014.

Stein, Joel. "The Me Me Me Generation: Why Millennials Will Save Us All." *TIME*. 20 May 2013 TIME, Inc. Wordpress.com VIP, 15 Oct. 2014. Web.

Talburt, Susan, and Nancy Lesko. "A History of the Present of Youth Studies." *Keywords in Youth Studies: Tracing Affects, Movements, Knowledges*. Eds. Nancy Lesko and Susan Talburt. New York: Routledge, 2012. Print.

"The Oxford Dictionaries Word of the Year 2013 Is… | OxfordWords Blog." *OxfordWords Blog*. N.p., n.d. Web. 12 Dec. 2014.

Tra_lalaaa. "Selfies." *Urban Dictionary*. N.p., 30 Aug. 2013. Web. 14 Dec. 2014.

Wa143aaaaah. "Selfies." *Urban Dictionary*. N.p., 22 Apr. 2005. Web. 12 Dec. 2014.

Wilson, Chris. "The Selfiest Cities in the World: TIME's Definitive Ranking." *TIME* 10 Mar. 2014 TIME, Inc. Wordpress.com VIP, 15 Oct. 2014. Web.

Transiciones: Pathways of Latinas and Latinos Writing in High School and College

Todd Ruecker
Logan: Utah State UP, 2015. 240 pp.

Reviewed by Brad Jacobson
University of Arizona

At first glance, Todd Ruecker's *Transiciones: Pathways of Latinas and Latinos Writing in High School and College* might seem a strange fit for a review in *Community Literacy Journal*. It is, after all, a study of high school to college transitions with a primary focus on classroom writing experiences. However, readers of *CLJ* will appreciate Ruecker's capacious approach to this important literacy transition, as he works to construct the networks of relationships and sponsors that support or hinder the transition for each student. In doing so, he calls for a more complex understanding of literacy transitions that can help shift the popular discourse from a focus on deficits, in which Latina/o students fail, to one of how institutions can better serve these traditionally underserved students. Following others in literacy studies, Ruecker believes institutions can and must change,  and he seeks to "imagine the ways high schools and universities can facilitate Latina/o student transitions into a more economically successful life" (147). Because of an action research approach that extends beyond only what takes place within classrooms, his findings offer possibilities for ways universities can better engage communities as well as how community organizations can support students as they engage the challenges of the college writing transition. Ruecker's work holds great value for all readers interested in supporting the success of college-going students.

As Ruecker explains in Chapter 1, a re-examination of mainstream instructional practices at the college level is necessary because the demographics of incoming college students no longer represent the "typical" white, middle-class, English-speaking student living on campus. Brief descriptions of the student participants in this ethnographic study help to support the statistical assertions offered. While all seven student participants attended the same high school in the border town of El Paso, Texas, they each brought different resources, abilities, and histories. Only one, for example, self-reported English as his first language. While some were educated in U.S. schools from K–12, one student reported starting as late as 8th grade. One of the participants traveled across the border from Mexico every day for his education. These brief histories will be familiar to readers with experience working in border regions.

To engage the complexity of the literacy transition across institutions for these students from ethnically and linguistically minoritized backgrounds, Ruecker draws from Tara Yosso's theory of community cultural wealth, which reinterprets Pierre Bourdieu's notions of habitus and capital through a Critical Race Theory (CRT) lens. As Ruecker explains, Yosso's work challenges the deficit perspective that students lack the proper capital or habitus for success, as she begins with the assumption that minority communities possess cultural wealth, and identifies six types of community cultural wealth: aspirational, linguistic, familial, social, navigational, and resistant capital (20). By adapting Yosso's model in his own analysis, Ruecker shifts from what could be a deficit-based analysis to an exploration of the ways in which students utilize their varied resources when they encounter challenges in the high school to college transition.

In Chapter 2, we are offered an overview of the differing writing experiences offered across institutional contexts. The impact of standardized testing heavily influences writing instruction at Samson High School (SHS), a school serving predominantly low-income Latina/o students, leading to a "culture of testing" that causes an ESL teacher to devote the majority of class time to test preparation materials (31). The value placed on student test achievement leads to limited writing opportunities for students in mainstream (non-AP) classes until senior English. Outside factors also influence writing instruction at the local community college. With five course schedules and teaching loads with multiple preparations, instructors have little time to innovate or bring an outdated curriculum based on the rhetorical modes in line with current disciplinary thinking. In contrast, Borderlands University (BU), a land-grant institution with a new writing program director and an influx of funding, hosts a transformed writing program with a new first-year writing curriculum focusing on building situated literacies. While Ruecker clearly implies a preference for this model, his purpose here is not to make judgments, but rather to show that at each institution external factors led to disparate writing opportunities for students. These in-depth descriptions based on curriculum recovery, observations, and interviews offer important insights into the potential literacy paths of students. These differences become an important lens for understanding the importance of community capital in writing transitions.

The next four chapters include the case studies, organized by the degree of success in the student's transition. For each case study, Ruecker offers a holistic description of the student, including personal and academic histories, describes writing experiences in high school and the first year of college, and concludes with a visual map and analysis of the student's resource network. Ruecker takes an action research stance and becomes a part of his participants' lives and academic transition. Whether he is helping a student acquire an internet connection at her home, responding to a text message about a paper at 10 p.m. on a Friday night, or copy-editing a draft in the hour before it is due, Ruecker places himself in the text as he participates in the experiences. This personal touch enlivens the narratives and provides a grounded ethos to his arguments. Interviews with the students, their teachers, and select administrators also provide depth that could not be gleaned by simply reading essays and evaluating curricula.

The value of Ruecker's methodology emerges first in Chapter 3, as Daniel struggles in his transition to community college. Daniel felt like he hadn't been pushed hard enough in high school, and his first-year composition (FYC) instructor accommodated him by allowing handwritten essays and going out of her way to follow up when he missed class. An interview shows a teacher who cares and tries to support students from diverse backgrounds, but Ruecker suggests that sometimes accommodating a struggling student can have unintended effects. In Daniel's case, it, "appeared to help … and hurt him," as Daniel himself blamed the low expectations of his high school teachers for the habits that he brought to college, and admitted that his overly supportive FYC instructor led to laziness (51). Only by triangulating this data among interviews, observations, and high school and college curricula could Ruecker come to such a nuanced claim that challenges teachers and administrators to critically reflect on our own practices.

In Chapter 4, we learn from narratives of two students who faced challenges but succeeded well enough in their first year to be considered on track. We see the importance of sponsorship outside the classroom, as both students draw from community networks of capital as they navigate the college transition. For example, Bianca gains both financial and emotional support from her church, one of the few places where she interacts with college graduates. She also gains sponsorship from the College Assistance Migrant Program (CAMP) at the state university, a support program for the children of migrant workers that includes some funding and summer programming including mandatory tutoring and study hours. Bianca was awarded with legal guardianship of her younger siblings after her mother was deported when she was a junior in high school, and an aunt stepped in to watch her siblings while Bianca participated in the summer program. These support networks were essential for Bianca's success; without them, college would not be possible. Similarly, Yesenia actively seeks support from teachers, instructors, tutors, and Ruecker as she navigates her transition. Once fearful of asking her eighth grade teacher to slow down even when she didn't fully understand English, Yesenia adapts well to college writing by drawing from her resources. Through these narratives we see the benefit of Ruecker's resistance to deficit-based analysis. One could view the participant's respective situations through what they lack—inadequate preparation from their high school, family responsibilities that could impinge on academic time, financial struggles—but a focus on community cultural wealth demonstrates the ways in which extracurricular resources can be just as influential to success.

The "smooth transitions" in Chapter 5 show students with well-developed networks of capital that serve to mitigate their challenges. Carolina arrived in U.S. schools in the eighth grade with little English ability, but a strong support network, including a supportive mother and a local Catholic community center. Carolina's support network offered homework help, tutoring, and computer classes, all of which helped her to build a strong academic foundation and some of the interpersonal skills necessary for college success. Initially shy and soft-spoken, Ruecker reports that Carolina "came across as a different person" after a few weeks of college (101). Out-of-school sponsorship, including a school leadership group that travelled to Washington, D.C. in the summer before her first year, helped her gain confidence in her communication skills and abilities to take on challenges. Ruecker implies that these sources of capital, in addition to Carolina's motivation and work ethic, allow her to succeed despite challenges.

It will not surprise most *CLJ* readers that Ruecker locates no silver bullet, no one particular resource that will secure a successful transition. In Chapter 6 we meet Paola, a student who faces many challenges, but succeeds in her first semester at community college. Initially uncertain about attending college and known as a rebellious student, Paola embraces the learning process, checking out books from the library and reporting that she did all the reading for her classes. Over winter break, however, Paola seems to lose her motivation. She moves in with her boyfriend, spending the weekends with him in Juárez. With limited internet access, she was forced to complete all of her homework on Sunday nights, leaving her exhausted and unprepared for Monday classes. She dropped all of her courses in the February of her second semester. Her story illustrates the "unpredictable nature of students' paths to and through college" (138) and shows that interpersonal networks impact students in multiple ways. Paola's story also serves to remind readers that the writing transition is only one of many factors in successful transitions to higher education, a point Ruecker returns to frequently in the final two chapters.

Ruecker admirably brings the case studies together in Chapter 7, titled "Contextualizing Transitions to College." He synthesizes the findings into a few key takeaways: First, the participants in this study were not prepared for college writing; none of them had experience writing the kinds of analytical essays they were expected to write in college. Next, he draws on Bourdieu to discuss the roles of habitus and capital in the institutional transition, using the term "hysteresis" to describe the lag that occurs when a person's habitus is slow to adapt to a new environment (143). Through this lens, we can see how some of the participants appear to have developed the college-going habitus in high school, while others did not have this same habitus, but their strong networks of community capital helped them to work through the hysteresis and build the college-going habitus over the course of their first year. However, as Paola's story demonstrates, "any theory of transition, such as Bourdieu's, is always limited by the complexity of human lives" (144). While Ruecker's research illuminates the importance of sponsors like church organizations, community networks, and scholarship programs in the literacy transition from high school to college, he reminds us that he was not able to stop three of his participants from dropping out of college, and he calls on other teachers and sponsors to "recognize that there are limits to what we can accomplish" (153).

Chapter 8 is a call to scholars, administrators, and literacy educators to consider ways to encourage institutional change that can better serve all students. First, Ruecker offers suggestions for instruction that would benefit linguistic minority students. He calls for a renewed focus on written feedback in an effort to improve scaffolding the development of students, as the students in this study did not receive sufficient feedback to help them develop skills quickly. Ruecker also advocates for more opportunities to build on the multiple literacies students bring by conducting cross-cultural rhetorical analyses or even providing bilingual courses. But Ruecker also recognizes that "what goes on beyond our classrooms matters much more," and calls on those working in writing instruction and administration "to work for much broader and ambitious transformations beyond their institutions" (156). He proposes service-learning and community-engaged pedagogy as one way to make visible the university-community relationship and increase engagement among students.

The institution itself, then, must change. In a recent retrospective on Deborah Brandt's *Literacy in American Lives*, Eli Goldblatt and David Joliffe suggest that "sponsors [of literacy] may have to undergo transformations they neither expect nor welcome" if they wish to engage with "groups not originally included in their charters or mission" (128). Ruecker's engaging, carefully researched ethnographic study serves to support this claim and act as a call to action. His work calls on scholars, teachers, and literacy practitioners to continue to push institutions toward change in order to better support the literacy transitions and life opportunities of Latina/o students.

Works Cited

Goldblatt, Eli, and David A. Joliffe. "*The Unintended Consequences of Sponsorship.*" *Literacy, Economy, and Power: Writing and Research after "Literacy in American Lives."* Ed. John Duffy, Julie Nelson Christoph, and Eli Goldblatt. Carbondale, IL: Southern Illinois UP, 2014. 127–35. Print.

Negotiating a Perilous Empowerment: Appalachian Women's Literacies

Erica Abrams Locklear
Athens: Ohio University P, 2011. 254 pp.

Review by Jessica Pauszek
Syracuse University

In the years since Jacqueline Jones Royster's seminal work *Traces of A Stream: Literacy And Social Change Among African American Women* (2000), scholars interested in literacy, identity, and social change have continued to pursue ways to include the voices of women who have previously been underrepresented within scholarly work. Indeed, these recovery projects—often considered part of a revisionist enterprise—represent important examples for those interested in the literary and rhetorical practices of women who have been overlooked based on gendered, ethnic, and socioeconomic identities. Illustrating this, scholars have developed a range of archival, rhetorical, and interview projects that uncover women as historical subjects who represent the myriad ways women develop and use rhetorical skills and literacies. For instance, in *Refiguring Rhetorical Education: Women Teaching African American, Native American, and Chicano/a Students, 1865–1911*, Jessica Enoch describes female teachers who contested the normative educational structures that oppressed marginalized groups and, rather, developed pedagogical strategies that encouraged civic participation. In another recovery project, *Beyond the Archives*, Gesa Kirsch describes the role of women who participated in a male-dominated sphere as physicians and civic advocates in the 19th century. In the same book, Wendy Sharer illustrates a new understanding of uncovering voices when she finds scrapbook examples of even her own grandmother's engagement with political literacies. These examples represent just some of the important work that has emerged in order to uncover and reframe the literate and rhetorical legacies of women from multiple subject positions.

Erica Abrams Locklear's book *Negotiating a Perilous Empowerment: Appalachian Women's Literacies* adds a unique contribution to these discussions by focusing on the literacies of women from Appalachia—a region, she argues, too-often characterized by a deficit framework. That is, Locklear challenges the gendered, regional, and classed stereotypes that represent women in Appalachia as "illiterate," "hillbillies," "Other," or "lesser"; instead, she shows the complexity of literacy acquisition and use for women from this community and confronts simplistic binary thinking that forms from stereotypes. Locklear provides valuable examples of how female writers and female characters negotiate identity through her critical analysis of fiction and nonfiction texts about Appalachia by Harriette Simpson Arnow, Linda Scott DeRosier, Denise Giardina, and Lee Smith, while also providing interview transcripts. In her analysis, Locklear uses these diverse examples of fictional characters and the real women writers who created them in order to explore the range of effects of literacy development, including the rejection of literacy some women chose to maintain their identity, the loss of cultural heritage they sustain, and the existing conflicts and opportunities that occur throughout the process.

Locklear's book is comprised of five main chapters, including the transcriptions of interviews with Linda Scott DeRosier and Lee Smith, and an introduction and epilogue. The introduction in particular contextualizes Appalachian women's literacies in relation to important questions surrounding ethnicity, social status, and geographic location that would be extremely beneficial for scholars who work at the nexus of literacy and identity with other marginalized populations. Chapters 2–5 function as a separate analysis of an Appalachian author and their text, while ultimately combining as a representative account of the social, emotional, and educational effects of literacy use for Appalachian women. While it is important not to conflate these accounts, there are many overlapping struggles that these women faced, most notably the negotiation of self and identity in their literacy development. *Negotiating a Perilous Empowerment* centers on the claim that literacy is neither static nor neutral. Rather, as the title suggests, the goals are to examine its complex—even contradictory—nature as both perilous and empowering, vexing and authorizing, for Appalachian women. In this way, Locklear argues that literacy—both as a term and process of development—is contentious for these women, and "often results in the constant negotiation of self-identity," particularly in ways that cause women to sacrifice a piece of themselves in order to gain literacy (2). Ultimately, Locklear claims that through her book "we can better understand the saturation of illiteracy stereotypes, the effects of those misconceptions on Appalachian people, and the subsequent empowerments and perils mountain women encounter when gaining new literacies" (53). Indeed, Locklear's argument successfully renders the complexities of literacies affected by gender, class, and region and shows how women navigate these positions.

In Chapter 1, Locklear sets up her discussion on how Appalachia is often described through deficit framings. Here, Locklear shows how these negative discourses circulated through mediums such as documentaries (*A Hidden America: Children of the Mountains*), books (*Moonlight Schools for the Emancipation of Adult Illiterates*), newspaper cartoons, and even through regional writers themselves who were "invested in securing the image of Appalachia as a fixed entity, one to be kept in its place as a politically useful repository of social aid" (24). In this chapter, Locklear effectively shows how these historical portrayals relied on Appalachia as "other" and, thus, were dangerous in their framing. However, similar to the revisionist work of the scholars previously mentioned, Locklear challenges this destructive scaffolding throughout her book, as she examines and uncovers both affordances and limitations of literacy for Appalachian women.

In Chapter 2, Locklear turns her focus to *The Dollmaker*, a 1954 novel written by Harriette Simpson Arnow. Using this text, Locklear develops an expansive discussion of literacies "that exten[d] beyond the technical ability to read and write" (57), in order to include discourses and literacy skills that female characters deploy at home (letter writing, whittling abilities, reciting Bible verses, and mothering techniques) and at school, where more traditional literacy-learning occurs. The Nevels family, created by Arnow, resides in Kentucky but moves to Detroit, where they suddenly realize the different cultural and social values between these spaces. For instance, Locklear notes that only upon moving does the family recognize the varying discourses they use and what literacies are privileged in each place. Although Locklear draws from work by James Paul Gee and Paulo Freire in order to develop a discussion about class-consciousness and the movement between discourses, she argues that Arnow's book suggests something different about literacy attainment where "no manner of compromise between mountain and city-based literacies appears" (58). While this chapter delivers powerful examples of the conflicts that emerge because of variations in discourse and literacy, it relies almost exclusively on close readings of Arnow's text to illustrate this work. This is a valuable textual model, but for those unfamiliar with Arnow's book and its scope as a fictional representation, it might be difficult to respond to and situate this argument in subsequent work.

Chapter 3 provides a particularly enlightening analysis of Linda Scott DeRosier's memoir writing, *Creeker: A Woman's Journey*, nonfiction work *Songs of Life and Grace*, and her personal experiences as an Appalachian woman and academic. Through the textual analysis and interview, Locklear powerfully illustrates the stakes that women from Appalachia face, most often resulting in some loss of their cultural heritage. For example, we learn DeRosier has incurred losses with her home identity as the "price that [she] pays for entrance into the academic community," especially in the form of "distinctive (and cherished) cultural markers that identify her as Appalachian, particularly her mountain speech patterns" (94, 109). Here, Locklear considers the socialization that occurs as DeRosier blends her Appalachian identity with the texts she creates in order to "overturn inaccurate assumptions that inevitably portray mountain people as ignorant, socially inept, and lesser" (95). This blending of academic and personal identities is simultaneously productive *and* challenging in DeRosier's experiences, as her personal life is infused with Appalachian histories and values that inform her work but also create tension when added to traditional academic inquiries that privilege standard academic patterns of speech and writing.

The focus of chapter 4 revolves around the work and life experiences of West Virginian author Denise Giardina. Here, Locklear argues that Giardina's work provides a representative instance of the challenges women face in combatting negative Appalachian stereotypes while also using her book *The Unquiet Earth* to "encourag[e]… readers to rethink their own notions of mountain illiteracy" (152). In fact, Locklear explains that the first limitation many people face, including Giardina, is the very absence of Appalachian women's writing in their lives, combined with destructive portrayals of their lives in the media. One character, Jackie, functions as a mouthpiece to show readers how moving into a new geographic location (from West Virginia to Washington D.C.) also forces her into a new discourse community, where she incurs a sense of cultural displacement. The geographic move parallels the sense of emotional loss that Jackie (and Giardina) feel when they move away from their home and realize that coming back to Appalachia will never be the same. Yet, there are benefits from this departure from their home community, as it is only through moving that they discover the agency that allows them to articulate their experiences as Appalachian women to a more public audience. As Locklear argues, Giardina's book "demonstrates how writing fiction allows her to write about both the personal loss she has incurred from gaining new literacies and the destruction and devastation caused by unethical coal mining practices [in West Virginia]" (145). In a sense, this fictional work by Giardina is a testimony of the difficulties of literacy acquisition and the negotiation of discourse communities.

The final chapter draws from Lee Smith's novels, such as *On Agate Hill, Fair and Tender Ladies, and Oral History*, in addition to a personal interview with Locklear. Locklear argues that these texts represent the ways in which Appalachian women use private writing, such as letters, as a form of public authorship. The oscillation between private and public spheres allows Smith's characters to participate in the creation of a counter-narrative—one that problematizes skewed notions of Appalachia as illiterate. Rather, through techniques of epistolary writing and oral history, Smith provides accounts of mountain life through characters who represent the changes women face when they gain new literacy and rhetorical skills. This chapter delves into the celebratory nature of writing for women who want their voice heard but also reinforces what Smith calls a "painful distancing" that often happens when women write about their community (211). While Smith agrees with the need for this work to happen, it also brings Locklear's main argument to the fore: that literacy use and development is, indeed, both perilous *and* empowering.

To be sure, there are many useful points in Locklear's book for those interested in thinking about the intersection of identity and literacy acquisition that strongly revolves around geographic location, gendered roles, and socioeconomic background. This book is groundbreaking in a move to combat the lack of representation (and marginalized portrayals) of Appalachian women's literacies throughout the years. Locklear skillfully crafts her argument about the perils and benefits of literacy attainment, while simultaneously creating a structure that relies on other female Appalachian authors who give voice to Appalachian women and participate in this representation through interviews. Therefore, her methods seem to enact a means of inclusion of multiple voices. Of course, while the focus on five writers is not exhaustive (nor should it be), Locklear gathers these perspectives in order to represent, and illuminate, the richness of Appalachian identity.

The intricate focus of this book is both a strength and challenge when thinking about its use for other scholars. This book blends discussions of literacy from standpoints that are suited for rhetoric and composition and also geared for a literature audience interested in close readings. It seems unique that Locklear relies intensely on fictional stories, which might prove difficult for expanding this work, if readers are unfamiliar with the texts used. Still, this book represents valuable stories of women who defy how literacy is understood and represented in texts on Appalachia, as well as evinces both the struggles and joys connected with literacy. For those particularly interested in revisionist methodologies, there are key mentions of alternative literacy sites developed in Appalachia, such as the Moonlight Schools and the Hindman Settlement School in Kentucky that Locklear argues have "informed contemporary discussions about literacy depictions in literature" (31). At the start of this review, I mentioned current projects that are shaping the field from a revisionist historiographical standpoint. Although, this is not the only way to read Locklear's book, it dovetails nicely with these discussions in rhetoric and composition and provides another fruitful example of how we can redefine and rethink literacy when we uncover narratives that have previously been located at the margins.

Producing Good Citizens: Literacy Training in Anxious Times

Amy J. Wan
Pittsburgh: U of Pittsburgh Press, 2014. Print. 232 pp.

Review by Daniel Bernal
University of Arizona

Strong in theory, rich in history, and far-reaching in its implications, *Producing Good Citizens* will soon become a staple for scholars, activists, and pedagogues alike who are interested in the complicated intersections of literacy and citizenship. In this historicized work, Amy Wan explores three main sites of citizenship training during the 1910s and 1920s—federally-sponsored immigrant Americanization programs, union-supported worker education training, and college-mandated first-year writing courses. Wan's book starts with a brief introduction to citizenship theory, moves into archival research of each training site, and concludes with applications of her methodology to present anxieties over citizenship, particularly in relation to the Patriot and DREAM Acts. Through her book, Wan complicates  citizenship as a discursive construct and demonstrates the limits of what literacy—and citizenship—can do for students as well as "the limitations put upon students by not only the idea of citizenship, but also its legal, political, and cultural boundaries" (178). Wan's powerful, timely argument and her final challenge to educators and scholars alike should not be ignored. Together, Wan invites us to consider what is meant by the invocation of citizenship in the classroom, to analyze the habits of citizenship that are encouraged by our practices, and to connect our citizen-making processes to other more politically and materially situated notions of citizenship.

In her use of "citizenship," Amy Wan builds on Danielle Allen's *Talking to Strangers* (2004), Barbara Cruikshank's *The Will to Empower* (1999), and Bryan Turner's introduction to *Citizenship and Social Theory* (1993). Wan, along with these scholars, expands the concept of citizenship from mere legal status to a "kind of credential with legal and cultural purchase" (6). In this manner, Wan justifies the exploration of citizenship construction in not only legal spaces, but also in classrooms, workplaces, and community spaces. She cites Harvey Graff's *The Literacy Myth* (1979) and Deborah Brandt's *Literacy in American Lives* (2001), assessing that, while literacy might deem an individual worthy of certain resources (i.e. passing first-year composition in order to graduate) it in no way guarantees social, economic, or political access. While this tendency to falsely conflate what Sharon Crowley describes as the "economic inequality and racial discrimination with a literacy problem" (qtd. in Wan, 7) might seem obviously erroneous, Wan is interested in its origins, pervasiveness, and rhetorical power. Ultimately, she concludes that this "literacy hope" serves to perpetuate systemic inequality.

Nevertheless, the invocation of citizenship production is also constantly leveraged to justify the usefulness of higher education, and especially the writing classroom. In this way, the ideals of citizenship support literacy instruction by proving that students are becoming the right kind of citizens who are doing the right kind of learning. Citizenship is referenced in student learning goals precisely because education is recognized as one of the traits of citizenship demonstrated by good and useful citizens. For example, Kathleen Yancey in her 2009 NCTE report calls for compositions that "foster a new kind of citizenship" (7). Yancey desires to empower students, "citizen writers" (1), to use twenty-first century writing skills to take action in a digital world. Wan also references other scholars such as Ellen Cushman (1998), Elizabeth Ervin (1997), and Michele Simmons (2007) who similarly characterize the writing classroom as a space that can "reinvigorate democratic and participatory citizenship through writing that relates to the public" (Wan 21). But Wan takes issue with these high-sounding arguments. She asserts that this undefined and "ambient awareness" (22) of citizenship plays a role in shaping the types of citizens that are produced. She writes, "The desired skills—public writing, public engagement, citizen critique, critical literacy, or technology—become inextricably, although often silently, linked to the imagined ideal of the 'good citizen'" (22). This is dangerous because educators' subconscious and unsifted views of what kind of people students should become may "conceal other ways of being a citizen" (Wan 22). Wan's work attempts to get at the roots of this ambient awareness of citizenship as civic engagement and provides a brief literature review of citizenship theory, drawing particularly from T.H. Marshall's right's oriented perspective of citizenship (1950), Judith Shklar's *American Citizenship* (1998), and Linda Bosniak's "Denationalizing Citizenship" (1976). Through these scholars, Wan calls into question the ambient understanding of citizenship, complicates the popular notion that citizenship is an achievable status (through literacy), and analyzes the view that it provides equal political standing and access to resources. Ultimately, she attempts to bring together the "theoretical good of citizenship with the material and political ... [by] looking at literacy *as a habit of citizenship* and considering how literacy teaching helps to construct this habit" (32). Wan's "habits of citizenship" approach broadens the scope of her investigation, allowing her to recognize both the direct habits instilled by literacy—like civic participation or good work habits—and the indirect influence of literacy on an individual's accessing of certain privileges of citizenship including political, social and economic access.

In chapter 2, Wan explores the individualistic, worker-citizens produced by federal Americanization programs in the early 20th century. She argues that the rhetorics of assimilation, patriotism, and citizenship promoted by such literacy training spaces worked to assuage predominant fears about the influx and perceived corrupting influence of immigrants, who were now emigrating in larger numbers and from areas other than Western Europe. One such 1918 federal textbook reads as follows: "I come to the evening school to speak American English. It means a better opportunity and a better home for me in America. It means a better job for me. It means a better chance for my children. It means a better America. I shall do my part in making a better America" (qtd. in Wan, 56). Lessons such as this one designed to teach literacy also inevitably carried habits of citizenship, transforming immigrants into citizen-workers who were "punctual, followed the company rules, and did not agitate against the factory owner" (68); in short, workers who would contribute much to the country, assimilate culturally, and be exploited. But Wan also demonstrates another consequence of this type of instruction—a brand of individualism. She writes, "With literacy as a crucial aspect of their training for citizenship, immigrants learned a kind of individualism, making them solely accountable for whether or not they could gain full citizenship. … Placing responsibility on individual actions and desires allowed for any poor treatment of new citizens to be concealed, making it the fault of the individual who did not fulfill citizenship's cultural requirements" (70). Throughout the final chapters of her book, Wan demonstrates how this intricate connection between individual prosperity, literacy, and citizenship has become embedded in the American psyche. And, of particular interest to scholars in our field, Wan explores how these notions of individualism live on in current iterations of literacy hope and equality narratives, evidenced in the rhetoric surrounding the DREAM Act.

In contrast to the individually-achieving, hard-working citizens created through Americanization programs, chapter 3 explores how workers' education programs teach literacy to cultivate a different type of citizenship. Wan cites extensively from labor newspapers and other publications put out by the International Ladies' Garment Workers' Union (ILGWU) and demonstrates that labor education imagined a more collaborative and intelligent type of citizen, characterized by civic responsibility to fellow workers. This vision of workers as members of a community with shared goals contrasts greatly with the highly individualized political and economic entities created by Americanization programs. Wan historicizes these goals within the framework of social anxiety—namely industrialization, mass production, and the changing roles of workers. Similarly, she explores how the unions used these programs to further the their goals: "the cultivation of leadership in the ranks, the recruitment of more educated workers leading to a stronger and larger labor movement, and the acquisition of intellectual equality with those in power such as bosses and politicians" (110). In this way, while workers' education attempted to expose assumptions about the equality of citizenship, they explicitly created the type of worker-citizens useful to the unions. Of particular interest to Wan is the union's orientation towards civic participation for a communal good. She argues that this movement perhaps sets the precedent of literacy training for critical literacy (110), but is hesitant to apply this type of thinking to contemporary writing classrooms.

University literacy instruction in the early twentieth century, as Wan explores in Chapter 4, arises out of similar societal anxieties and "illustrates how the concept of citizenship was used to construct a burgeoning middle class" (114). Wan's work challenges Robert Connors' (1997) characterization of this period in education as a "consolidation period" (Wan 119). She contends that this period, "rather than one of consolidation, actually reflects the flux and turmoil found outside the college classroom" (Wan 119). Specifically, Wan focuses on the English classroom as a citizen-making space, which she asserts "has strong roots in the period around the First World War with its anxieties about the growing number of immigrants and shifting work expectations" (123). Her analysis of NCTE publications shows a movement away from teaching literature and other cultural texts, in favor of "teaching the communicative, intellectual, and ethical skills to be a self-governed citizen" (125). Taken in conjunction with the other case studies Wan has reviewed, this chapter demonstrates the production of a different sort of citizenship—primarily coming from the middle and upper classes, but a citizen concerned with both work and civic participation—in some ways a combination of the union member and immigrant-student. Wan argues that in this training site, while literacy is primarily seen as a tool for "future productivity" (114), students would also learn the "communicative, intellectual, and ethical skills needed to be a self-governed citizen" (125). In this vein, Wan analyzes how teachers in the 1910s and 1920s constructed classrooms as little republics, set stages for debates, and connected course content to the world—thereby preparing students for civic, and not only economic, participation. The writing classroom pledged to provide students with economic, political, social, and even spiritual benefits, which, in turn, provided legitimacy for the institutions.

Wan's final chapter fast-forwards to the present, demonstrating how equality narratives and versions of literacy hope are still prevalent today. She calls for a self-analysis of how educators define citizenship in the context of education and literacy training and argues that a nuanced understanding of citizenship can help us to negotiate the space between the traditional goals of liberal arts education and an increasingly vocational paradigm; between the collective goals of democracy and the private goals of access to high-paying jobs (155). But, while Wan starts by emphasizing the importance of education towards the creation of citizenship, she soon moves to the importance of citizenship in an individual's access to education through a discussion of the Patriot and DREAM Acts. She roots these legislations in cultural anxieties over immigration similar to those twentieth-century anxieties explored throughout her book and posits that the "DREAM Act reinforces the long-standing appeal of education and literacy as components of defining citizenship" (165). This section of her work is timely but far-too-short and therefore begs further research. Of particular interest to community literacy studies is Wan's suggestion that, in the vein of the immigrant-Americanization programs of chapter 2, the common narratives about the dreamers which focus on *individual* achievement against all odds, "rather than a larger, more meaningful overhaul of the way a nation defines its citizens … might undermine hopes for a less-punitive immigration policy" (169). Simply put, Wan argues that by publicizing individual "success stories" we invisibilize the larger social, economic, and political barriers to citizenship faced by immigrants, as well as overplay literacy and higher education as the preferred road to citizenship. This final example, along with Wan's charge to "teacher-citizens" (171), invites educators and scholars alike to weigh literacy's privileged role in citizenship-production against a more complicated, materially situated notion of citizenship in order to better understand all its consequences for our colleges, classrooms, and communities.

Creating Effective Community Partnerships for School Improvement: A Guide for School Leaders

Hazel M. Carter
New York: Routledge, 2013. 240 pp.

Review by Erika Dyk

North Dakota State University

Education reform is a constant in ongoing academic conversations; however, the tools and resources necessary for that reform can be daunting or simply remain in the abstract world of theory and not action. *Creating Effective Community Partnerships* walks readers through the concrete process of partnering with other educational institutions, stakeholders, and community organizations, showcasing concrete examples to match the principles it advocates. As the title suggests, Carter more overtly targets administrators and administrators-in-training; however, this book is helpful for other stakeholders too. She especially calls for institutions at all levels to take part in conversations about educational reform and to refrain from playing the often easy but fruitless "blame game." Carter ventures to break down not only the requisite aspects of beneficial collaboration between schools and communities, but to reflect on her own institutional location. She further seeks to change the way leaders imagine resources, to "think of the community as a logical partner in bringing about success for students, their families, and school staff" (Carter xix). She urges school leaders to be innovative and to delve into the larger community to provide the best learning opportunities for students, especially those considered at risk of school failure. Throughout the book, Carter writes in a direct, no-frills fashion, supporting and justifying practices with educational research. The book's appendix offers examples from the two projects that are the focus of the book, specifically she shows readers how to craft practical agendas, budgets, timetables, lessons, and professional development workshop offerings. Such an appendix becomes a valuable tool for readers who are serious about the nuts and bolts of community collaboration.

It is worth noting that Carter organizes the book around two community partnerships: a six-year, grant-funded program focusing on middle school students—to prepare them for educational transitions—and a high school-college partnership that is funded publicly. Furthermore, she aligns eleven of the twelve chapters with the

Educational Leadership Constituent Council (ELCC) standards, and provides a sample course syllabus in the preface if instructors wish to use it as a textbook. The short chapters and recurring features—such as reflective exercises and portfolio building activities—make Carter's book easily adaptable for classroom use. Reflective exercises challenge readers to apply the book's concepts to their own situations and the portfolio-building activities help readers to compile a working collection of their ideas. Some of the chapters also include a "lessons learned" section in which the author reflects upon unforeseen circumstances in her collaborative experience and offers concrete recommendations; in doing so, she skillfully models the reflection process that should be integral within community partnerships.

Chapter 1 establishes numerous problems educators face and connects these recurring difficulties to concrete actions community members can take. She also argues that we all need to be concerned about the "social costs" of educational problems. Carter also asserts that the issue with college retention rates is not simply the problem of higher education—this issue spans the entire educational process, K–16. Chapter 2 then sets forth scaffolding to help readers discern who would make an effective collaborative partner and what different levels of collaboration entail. Carter emphasizes the importance of a shared vision, not just "for educators, but for the community at large" (15), and identifies specifically the key strategies for building an "educational collaborative team" (18).

In chapter 3, Carter discusses the importance of intentionally creating structures for community collaboration by showcasing what collaboration looks like in real situations. Chapter 4 focuses on the transition from middle school to high school, calling for these institutions to collaborate on this transition. In Chapter 5, Carter continues to focus on at-risk students, recognizing that they are the ones least likely to transition to college, let alone struggle through the transition unless they have a robust support network. Chapter 6 specifically addresses partnering with parents and the community in urban areas, though surely her recommendations are applicable to rural schools as well. Parental involvement and community support structures are both key, Carter notes, but often missing for at-risk students. In Chapter 7, Carter focuses on the need for schools to seek funding from private foundations, providing a helpful annotated list of foundations offering educational grants and guiding readers through the grant-writing process. While private funding sources are valuable in our current political and economic climate, it is worth mentioning that public funding sources have historically provided the bulk of funding for educational institutions based on the concept that an informed citizenry is superior to an ignorant one.

Carter rightly emphasizes the importance of teachers maintaining a close learning relationship with students; of course this relationship becomes strained due to neoliberalism as class sizes expand and machine grading replaces teachers guiding students through the writing process. In chapter 8, she recognizes the imperative role of the classroom teacher and advocates that "[o]ne of the most promising strategies for improving schools is giving teachers more control of schools and of what occurs in the classroom" (97). Chapter 9 emphasizes the role of the collaborative leader and calls for a shift in educational culture. Carter maintains, "[a] school that does not have a culture of collaboration is not ready to receive [or extend] partnership programs" (114). Carter advocates for reading, writing, and study groups—of varied demographics—as one method to prepare a school for collaboration. Chapter 10 reflects on the results of student surveys from the college-readiness program. Carter also highlights the services offered to the students and argues for the importance of modifying collaborative programs to meet the needs of students deemed to be academically underprepared or otherwise at risk for failing school. Chapter 11 focuses on "Building Community through Professional Development," emphasizing the importance of teachers continually learning through grassroots teacher collaboratives to better guide students to success. Carter praises researcher Linda Darling Hammond's findings that "improving the expertise of teachers, dollar for dollar, results in far greater gains in student learning than do investments in tests, materials, or programs" (149). Chapter 12 reiterates the value of partnerships, advocates for administrators to recognize faculty who have leadership potential, and ends with a call to revolutionize the senior year of high school to partner with colleges and community organizations to help facilitate a better transition to the next phase of the student's development, writing, and learning.

Leaders, teachers, and community members, especially those new to community literacy work, can benefit from this book as it provides pragmatic recommendations to change systems that are failing educators and students alike. Carter's call to action entails becoming intentional about beginning and maintaining conversations with the key stakeholders involved in educational reform. Carter charts a course for how educational reform can be accomplished, recognizing that each situation and context will look a little different, especially when reflecting upon students', teachers', and community members' needs. While Carter acknowledges that this book is for all stakeholders, its primary target is school leaders. The two projects Carter features in this book highlight the need for strong leadership and the vision and management acumen necessary not only to fund but also to oversee changes to successful fruition. Having the right partnerships, people, and culture in place is imperative to this process—which may sometimes begin with the leaders, but is not possible to sustain without the rest of the organization understanding and working toward the same goal. While Carter provides a helpful foundation for why school and community partnerships need to exist, she also focuses significant time on workplace readiness and monetary loss if students do not finish school. The idea of citizenship was not always presented as overtly by Carter as it could have been, although undertones of citizenship are present. Thus, this book is most helpful for readers who want to engage in collective reform but aren't sure where to start. This book includes sections that might not be necessary for experienced leaders, but offers excellent resources to new leaders.

On the whole, Carter's book is teeming with resources and ideas and is ultimately a call to action, a call to leaders. However, the respect shown to all stakeholders, especially teachers, relies upon bottom-up approaches and methodologies. Perhaps this is because ultimately we are all leaders to some extent and we all must work together bring about the change we desire within our communities. As Carter maintains, collaboration cannot just be small projects here and there, though there is certainly nothing wrong with light-touch approaches to community building. Carter's book is an important, theoretically sound, and workable resource which would have powerful impacts if approached with a disposition of openness.

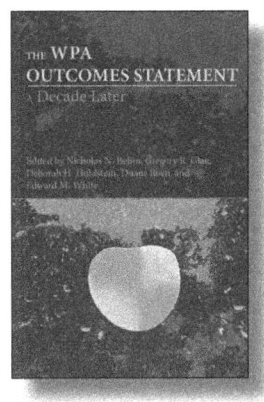

Congratulations to These Award Winners & WPA Scholars!

The WPA Outcomes Statement—A Decade Later
Edited by Nicholas N. Behm, Gregory R. Glau, Deborah H. Holdstein, Duane Roen, and Edward M. White
Winner of the Best Book Award, Council of Writing Program Adminstrators (July, 2015)

GenAdmin: Theorizing WPA Identities in the Twenty-First Century
Colin Charlton, Jonikka Charlton, Tarez Samra Graban, Kathleen J. Ryan, & Amy Ferdinandt Stolley
Winner of the Best Book Award, Council of Writing Program Adminstrators (July, 2014)

Mics, Cameras, Symbolic Action: Audio-Visual Rhetoric for Writing Teachers
Bump Halbritter
Winner of the Distinguished Book Award from *Computers and Composition* (May, 2014)

New Releases

First-Year Composition: From Theory to Practice
Edited by Deborah Coxwell-Teague & Ronald F. Lunsford. 420 pages.

Twelve of the leading theorists in composition studies answer, in their own voices, the key question about what they hope to accomplish in a first-year composition course. Each chapter includes sample syllabi.

A Rhetoric for Writing Program Administrators
Edited by Rita Malenczyk. 471 pages.

Thirty-two contributors delineate the major issues and questions in the field of writing program administration and provide readers new to the field with theoretical lenses through which to view major issues and questions.

www.parlorpress.com

DEPAUL UNIVERSITY

DEPARTMENT OF
WRITING, RHETORIC, & DISCOURSE

Master of Arts Degrees in
NEW MEDIA STUDIES
WRITING, RHETORIC, & DISCOURSE
with concentrations in
Professional & Technical Writing
Teaching Writing & Language

Graduate certificate in TESOL
Combined BA/MA in WRD

Bachelor of Arts in WRITING, RHETORIC, & DISCOURSE
Minor in **Professional Writing**

 facebook.com/DePaulWRD   @DePaulWRD

WRD.DEPAUL.EDU

www.ingramcontent.com/pod-product-compliance
Lightning Source LLC
Chambersburg PA
CBHW031334160426
43196CB00007B/690